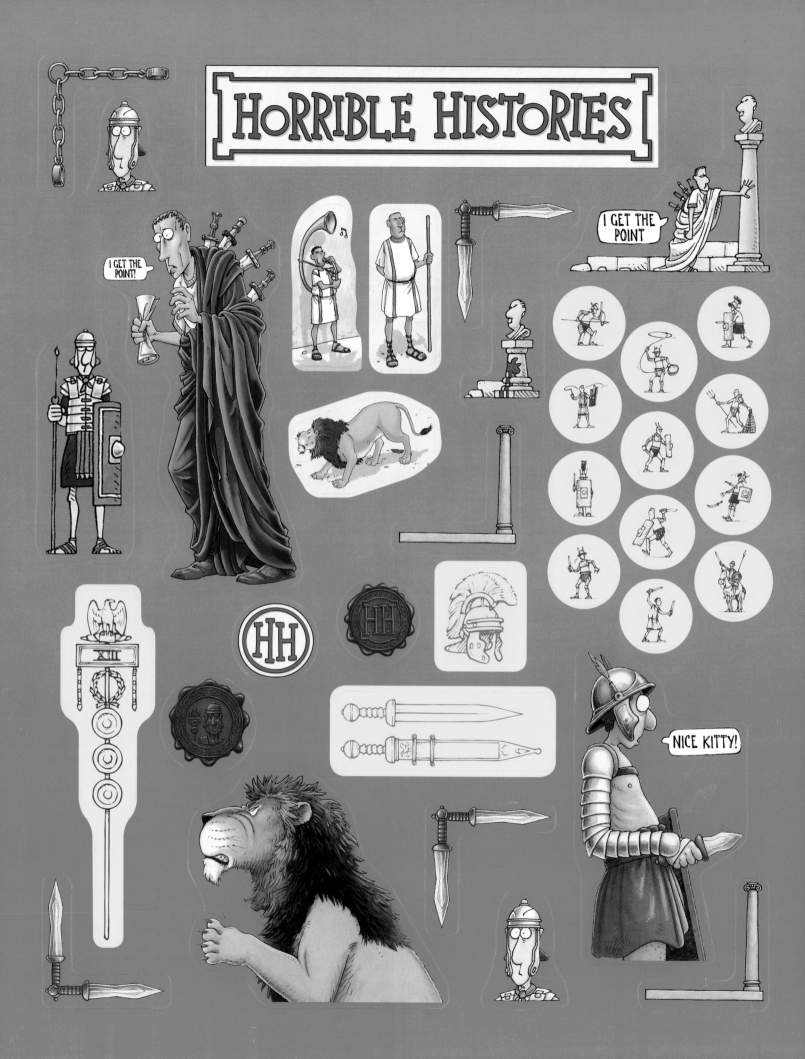

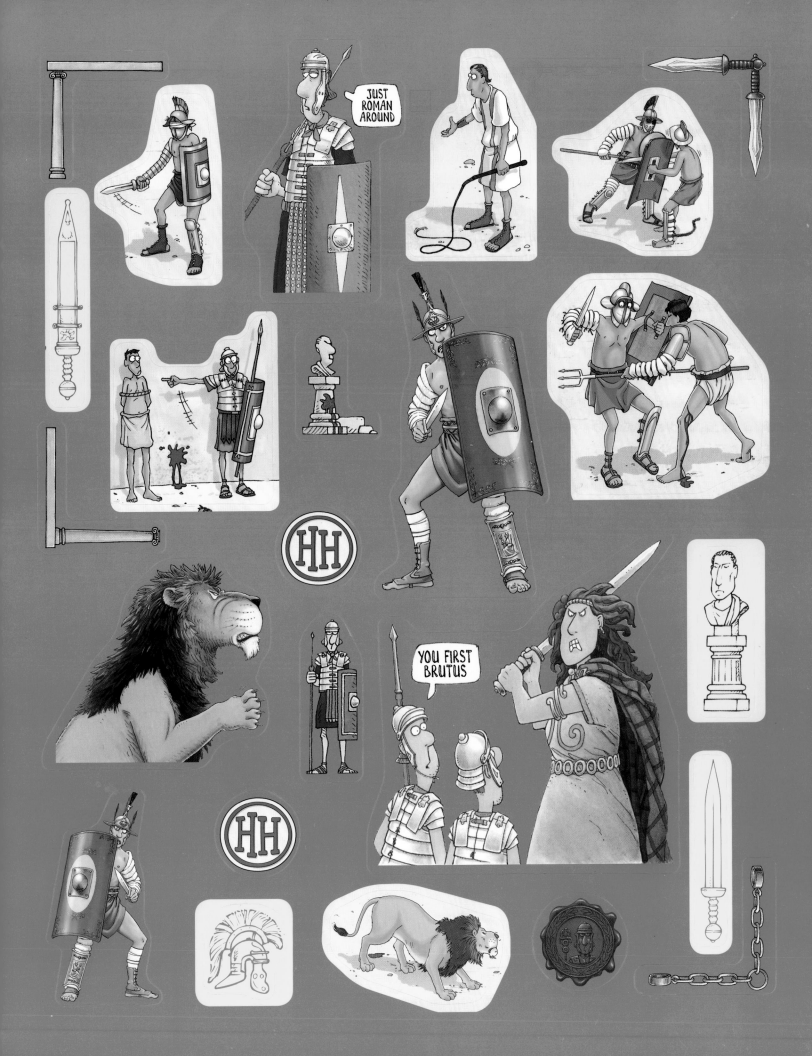

HORRIBLE HISTORIES

THE HORRIBLY HUGE BOOK

OF

AWFUL EGYPTIANS & RUTHLESS ROMANS

TERRY DEARY ILLUSTRATED BY MARTIN BROWN

SCHOLASTIC

Scholastic Children's Books
Euston House
24 Eversholt Street
London
NW1 1DB

A division of Scholastic Ltd
London ~ New York ~ Toronto ~ Sydney ~ Auckland
Mexico City ~ New Delhi ~ Hong Kong

The Awful Egyptians
First published in the UK by Scholastic Ltd, 2006
Text copyright © Terry Deary, 2006
Illustrations copyright © Martin Brown, Mike Phillips, 2006.

The Ruthless Romans
First published in the UK by Scholastic Ltd, 2003
Text copyright © Terry Deary, 2003
Illustrations copyright © Martin Brown, 2003

This compilation copyright © Scholastic Ltd, 2008

Some of the material in this book has previously been published in Horrible Histories: The
Awesome Ancient Quiz Book, The Rotten Romans Sticker Book, The Awesome Egyptians Activity
Book and The Wicked History of the World
Activities created and produced by The Complete Works, St Mary's Road, Royal Leamington Spa,
CV31 IJP.
Additional text by Dereen Taylor and Jenny Siklos.
Additional illustrations by Mike Phillips

ISBN 978 1407 10796 7

Printed and bound by Tien Wah Press Pte. Ltd, Malaysia

2 4 6 8 10 9 7 5 3 1

CONTENTS

In fond memory of
Rosemary Bromley, 1922–2005,
without whom Horrible Histories
would not have been written. TD

CONTENTS

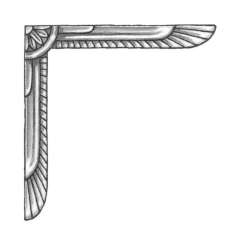

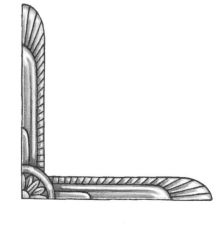

Introduction

The people of Ancient Egypt could be pretty horrible.

They just did not like the idea of dying and simply vanishing. They wanted to think there is a life after death. And to make sure they made it to that life, they had to stop their bodies going rotten.

I CAN'T ENJOY ME DINNER IF ME HAND DROPS OFF AND ME TEETH DROP OUT, CAN I?

Rich people could afford to have their bodies cleaned up and wrapped up to stop them going 'off' – a bit like when we put baked beans into a tin. The dead rich were turned into 'mummies'.

Of course, if you are going to take your body with you into the afterlife then you'll need all the things you had in this world: food, clothes, treasure and furniture.

The horrible bit was that some of the old kings wanted to take their servants and pets with them.

YOU CAN'T EXPECT A KING TO COOK AND CLEAN, CAN YOU?

So where would they find a pile of dead servants to take with them?

You wouldn't. There were no scrap-yards for dead second-hand servants. So they took LIVE servants and murdered them. Then they dropped them into the tomb with the dead king.

They did the same to poor palace pussy cats – they smacked them over the head and didn't paws to think about it.

This is the sort of foul fact that will give you nightmares. The terrifying tales in this book will haunt you like the curse of a mummy.

You do NOT want to hear what the Egyptians were REALLY like. Oh, no, you don't.

Oh very well. Here is the horrible history of those awesome ancients. Read it and see how lucky you are to be alive today, and not in evil Egypt…

Awful Egyptian timeline

The Egyptians are so-o-o very ancient that we don't really know where they came from. You could go on looking for answers till you're as old as a mummy (or as old as YOUR mummy).

But we do know that prehistoric people roamed around in North Africa, finding food. Then those people started to settle down next to the River Nile because it flooded regularly and made the land rich for growing crops.

Here is a rough timeline of what happened.

5500 BC Awesome Egyptian people begin to settle beside the River Nile. But they haven't invented the wheel yet – which is a bit of a drag!

3000 BC North and South Egypt unite under one king (or pharaoh), the start of a long line of rulers who will later build massive pyramids. The first pharaoh is known simply as 'Scorpion' – did he have a poison tale to tell? We don't know.

3000 BC Egyptian people invent writing around the same time as the Sumerians. Not only can we record history, we can have schools and history tests!

2650 BC The first pyramids are built in Egypt. You can see the point – it's there on the top. Pharaoh Djoser gets his people to build the

9

'Step' pyramid. These pharaohs are now 'gods' who will look after Egypt and its people.

1650 BC The Hyksos from Asia invade Egypt and take over the north. Where are those pharaoh gods when you need them?

1570 BC The Kushites from Sudan attack Egypt, but their king is killed.

1540 BC Egypt switches to burying its kings in tombs cut into rock. The grave robbers were breaking into those pyramids too easily.

750 BC The Kushites attack Egypt again. This time they win and they rule for 100 years. Those gods must have been on holiday at the time…

663 BC The Assyrians invade Egypt. You can't blame them – Egypt has been attacking Assyria for centuries. Assyrian King Ashurbanipal is a great but cruel ruler. He is driven out after 20 years.

539 BC The powerful Persians conquer Babylon then go on to take over Egypt. The Persians become ancient top dogs.

356 BC Alexander the Great is born in Macedonia, north of Greece. He will grow up to conquer Persia, Mesopotamia and Egypt from about 305 BC as part of his plan to take

over the world. The Greeks will rule for 300 years, making the peasants poorer and the royals richer.

30 BC The last Greek queen of Egypt, Cleopatra, kills herself and the Romans take over the country.

Phunny pharaohs

Around 5500 BC the awesome Egyptians moved into the land by the River Nile. Every year the river flooded and left lovely squidgy mud covering the fields for a few miles on either side – lovely squidgy mud that was good for growing crops.

The people of the Nile could usually grow enough food to live on – but they were always worried that one year the Nile would let them down and they'd all starve. So they invented gods and prayed that the gods would make the Nile flood.

Then along came some really clever people who said…

These really clever people became known as 'pharaohs' – probably because they had a 'fair-old' life with peasants slaving for them![1]

Top ten pharaohs

No one knows where the pharaohs came from. Maybe they were just the leaders of peasant tribes. But around 3150 BC one became so powerful that he was more than a head-man – he was a 'king' (or pharaoh).

In school you are all in little tribes called 'classes' with a leader called a 'teacher'. But how does one teacher get to rule all the other teachers and become a 'head'?

1 Nah, that's not true. 'Pharaoh' is the Egyptian word for 'Great House'. The peasants didn't dare speak the name of their king so they called him 'The Great House', which is a bit like a Brit calling the queen 'Mrs Buckingham Palace' or an American calling the president 'Mr White House'.

Some people say…

Hmmmm! That may be true for head teachers, but probably not for the pharaohs.

We don't know a lot about the early pharaohs, but there are a few bits of horrible history we have discovered about their powerful pasts.

Your teacher may even be able to pick up a few tips on how to be a head!

Here is a top ten of phoul pharaohs…

1 Narmer (ruled around 3150 BC)

Name means: 'The striking catfish'

How did he get to be pharaoh? By being super-cruel.

Pictures of Narmer show him holding a prisoner on the end of a rope … and the rope has been pushed through a hole in the prisoner's nose. Ouch. Who knows how Narmer got his power?

There are also pictures of his enemies lying on the ground – have they just nodded off? No, because they're headless – sort of noddle off.

But remember there were no sharp steel swords or axes in Egypt. Having your head cut off with a soft copper blade would be slower and more painful than a quick chop.

2 Djoser (ruled 2668–2649 BC)

Name means: 'Holy one'
Djoser built the first of the great pyramids then he died and was made into a mummy. His insides were packed into containers called canopic jars – one each for his liver, his stomach, his guts and his lungs. That's what happened to all mummies.

But Djoser was king of South Egypt and North Egypt. To keep the people in both parts of the country happy he had to be buried in two different tombs. His body was entombed in the north, and his canopic jars had their own temple 100 metres to the south.

He was buried with food to take to the afterlife, but imagine what would have happened when his spirit got hungry…

He'd have to go for a spooky stroll to the south temple, pick up his stomach, slap it back in, then go back to the north temple for his grub. When he'd finished he'd have to drop his stomach off at the south temple and … oh, you get the idea.

Imagine sitting down to your school dinner then realizing you have to cross the school playing fields and back to get your guts.

3 Khufu (ruled 2589–2566 BC)

Name means: 'He protects me'

Khufu has the biggest pyramid, the biggest statue and the biggest ships in Egypt.

After Khufu's death his son had two ships buried beside his great pyramid at Giza. The ships were found in 30-metre pits. The ships were over 40 metres long.

'Hang on!' I hear you cry. 'Hang onnnnn a minute!'

Of course there is a simple answer. The ships were taken apart before they were buried. What was found was a sort of ship kit pit[2].

The spirit of the ship would carry the spirit of Khufu to the afterlife. Of course we don't know why they were buried a few years after Khufu … or why there were two of them.

2 Try saying that with a mouth full of marshmallows. Bet you can't – even without the marshmallows.

16

4 Pepi II (ruled 2278–2184 or 2218)

Name means: 'Ka of Ra is powerful'

No one can agree how long Pepi II ruled. Some say sixty years, some say ninety, but most agree that he came to the throne when he was only six years old.

Was he interested in war? No.

Was he interested in pyramids and statues? No.

Did Pepi want a puppy? No.

He was only interested in getting a dwarf for his palace.

His army set off into Africa and reports came back that they had captured a pygmy. Little Pepi was wetting himself with excitement. He wrote a message to his general telling him how to treat the captured pygmy.

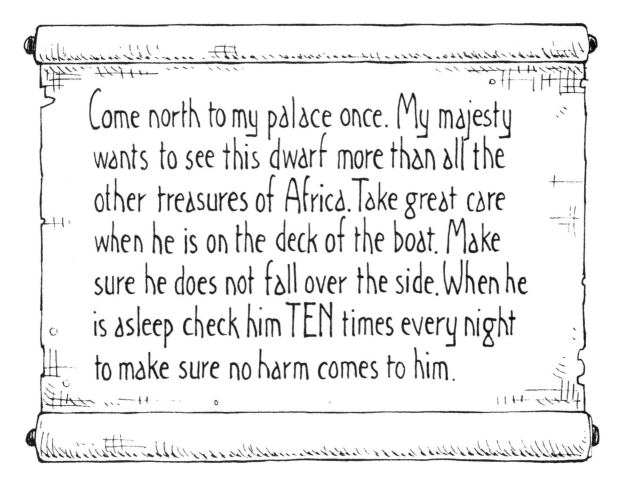

Come north to my palace once. My majesty wants to see this dwarf more than all the other treasures of Africa. Take great care when he is on the deck of the boat. Make sure he does not fall over the side. When he is asleep check him TEN times every night to make sure no harm comes to him.

The pygmy got there safely. Pepi was happy.

The one thing that bothered Pepi was flies. How did he deal with the problem? Here's how…

Clever Pepi.

But Pepi lived TOO long. Some say he lived to be a hundred years old.

Egypt needed a powerful ruler, not a wrinklie. Egypt almost fell apart when he died as princes fought for the throne.

5 Mentuhotep I (ruled 2060–2010 BC)

Name means: 'The god of war is satisfied'
After all the trouble Pepi II left behind, along came Mentuhotep. He sorted out the rebels by killing them.

So many soldiers died in Mentuhotep's battles that they invented the world's first war cemetery.

In the 1920s the American historian Herbert Winlock discovered a graveyard with sixty of Mentuhotep's soldiers. Soldiers had always been buried on the battlefield where they died, but these men had all been brought back from Nubia, hundreds of miles to the south. They were buried near the tomb of Mentuhotep who had sent them to die for him.

But who got the job of bringing back the sixty bodies? In the hot Egyptian sun they would have gone off very quickly and started to smell.

PHEW! MORE FLIES THAN A PEPI SLAVE

6 Senusret III (ruled 1870–1831 BC)

Name means: 'Man of goddess Wosret'

Just south of Egypt was Nubia. The people there were a problem from time to time. They enjoyed attacking Egypt and trying to steal its treasures.

Pharaoh Senusret III wrote down the way he dealt with them:

I SHOW NO MERCY. IF YOU ATTACK A NUBIAN HE WILL RUN AWAY. BUT IF YOU RUN AWAY HE WILL ATTACK YOU. THE NUBIANS ARE WRETCHES AND COWARDS. I KIDNAPPED THEIR WOMEN, I CARRIED OFF THEIR FRIENDS, I CUT OFF THEIR WATER, I KILLED THEIR BULLS, I CUT THEIR CORN AND BURNED IT

Nice man. The message is clear – don't mess with Senusret.

But Senusret was two metres tall. His methods may not have worked if he'd only been one metre tall.

7 Tao I (ruled around 1560 BC)

Name means: 'road, pathway'

Around 1650 BC the Hyksos people from Asia invaded Egypt and took over the north. The Egyptians went on ruling in the south.

The Hyksos won their battles because they had new weapons that the Egyptians had never seen – chariots and archers with bows and arrows.

The Hyksos leader Apepi I lived in Avaris in the north. He wrote a very odd letter to the Egyptian leader Tao at Thebes in the south.

It sounds as if he was trying to wind him up…

> I am angry, Tao. I cannot sleep at night in Avaris. Why not? Because I am disturbed by the roaring of the hippos at Thebes. I want you to do something about this at once ~ or else!

Avaris is 500 MILES from Thebes.

Sadly we don't know what Tao's reply was. But if Apapi was trying to start a fight then he succeeded.

Tao and his Egyptians rose up against the Hyksos. In time they would drive the Hyksos out of Egypt …. but Tao didn't live to see it.

His mummy was discovered at Deir el-Bahari in 1881. The skull showed terrible wounds…

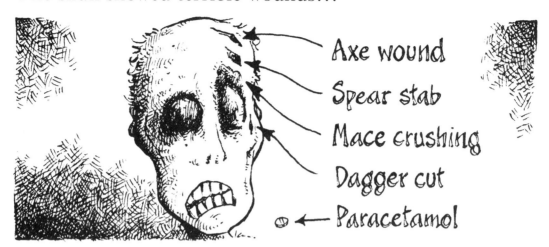

Axe wound
Spear stab
Mace crushing
Dagger cut
← Paracetamol

But the wounds were not the sort Tao would have got if he had been standing up and fighting – he was lying on his right side.

Was he knocked down and hacked? Or was he murdered in his sleep?

We'll never know.

AND I'LL NEVER KNOW EITHER!

8 Hatshepsut (ruled 1479–1457 BC)

Name means: 'Distinguished woman'
Hatshepsut was a bit odd because he was a actually a she – one of the few ancient Egyptian woman pharaohs. Pharaoh Tuthmosis III was supposed to rule, but he was only a child when his father died, so his bossy step-mother, Hatshepsut, helped him[3].

In the end she also helped herself – to the throne. She called herself pharaoh and did all the things that pharaohs did…

---

3 She was also his auntie – those royal ancients married anyone they took a fancy to – even members of their own family!

Hatshepsut decided that her father, Pharaoh Tuthmosis I, had wanted her to succeed to the throne. Carvings have been found in temples…

And she had the carvings changed to say…

She also changed carvings so they said SHE had driven out the invading Hyksos when really it had been her father. Power had definitely gone to her head…

Of course it couldn't last. Little Tuthmosis grew up to hate his step-mother. She died … and Tuthmosis may have had something to do with it.

NOT ME! SHE WAS CARVING UP A BOILED BABOON AND THE KNIFE SLIPPED. HONEST!

9 Tuthmosis III (ruled 1479–1425 BC)

Name means: 'Born of the God Thoth'

Tuthmosis officially came to the throne in 1479 BC, but he spent 22 years being ruled by his step-mother. So when he got the throne he tried to prove that he wasn't really such a wimp. He had stories carved in temples that said things like…

I have killed seven lions and twelve wild bulls all by myself

He also enjoyed killing elephants to get their ivory tusks. In one hunt he apparently killed 120 elephants[4].

But it took him twenty years to kill one step-mother.

10 Ramesses II – The Great (ruled 1279–1212 BC)

Name means: 'Re has finished him'

This 'great' warrior king made Egypt rich by invading other countries and stealing their treasures. But not all his victories were so great.

His biggest enemies were the Hittites. They were always attacking Egypt so Ramesses set off with a massive army to smash them once and for all.

He captured two spies and tortured them. They said…

Ramesses thought this was his chance to attack the Hittite city of Kadesh. It was almost impossible to capture because it was on an island.

Then he discovered that the spy had lied. The Hittite army was waiting for him in Kadesh – he'd walked into a trap.

Ramesses battled bravely to save his life but when he realized he was being beaten he made peace and went home. He then had the story of the Battle of Kadesh carved on temple walls.

4 One of his soldiers, Amenemhab, wrote that he chopped off the trunk of a live elephant while the Pharaoh watched. Tuthmosis rewarded him with three sets of clothes.

What story did they tell?

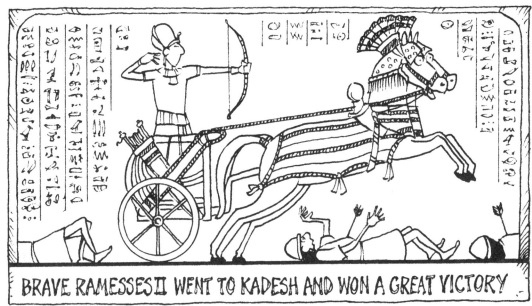

BRAVE RAMESSES II WENT TO KADESH AND WON A GREAT VICTORY

HE KILLED LOTS OF HITTITES WITH HIS OWN HAND

Er … a bit of a fib, your majesty[5]?

The pictures show how the Egyptians counted the enemy dead. They would lop a hand off each one and take them home to count them. That way a body could not be counted twice. The Egyptians knew how to do these things – you have to hand it to them.

5 The Hittites made their own carvings that gave their side of the story. The Hittites said Ramesses was the one who asked for peace. Who do YOU believe?

Did you know…?

In 1435 BC Pharaoh Tuthmosis III planned an attack on the city of Kadesh. He lined up his horses outside the city and the Hittite army did an odd thing. They sent out a mare to scare the Egyptians.

Why? Because the Egyptians were riding male horses. The sight of a female horse would send them charging off after her. The soldier Amenemhab boasted about what happened next…

That must have made the Egyptian horses a bit sad.

Bible bashing

The Hittites weren't Ramesses' only enemy. The Hebrews (Jews) suffered his brutal bullying. The Bible tells their story.

Ramesses made the Hebrews his slaves and forced them to build new temples and palaces for him. The Hebrew leader, Moses, begged Ramesses to set them free.

He tried ten times but Ramesses wouldn't budge. So God made the rivers run with blood as a punishment. Fish died, Egyptians couldn't drink, the river smelled rotten.

Then, in each Egyptian family, the oldest child died suddenly in the night. Ramesses changed his mind…

The Hebrews headed home … then Ramesses changed his mind AGAIN. He sent an army after the Hebrews.

They caught up with the slaves at 'the Sea of Reeds'. Then God helped the Hebrews again. He made a path through the sea for Moses and his people. When the Egyptian army tried to follow, God let the waters rush back and they were all drowned.

Of course Ramesses did NOT have this exciting story carved on the walls of his temples.

That's Ramesses the Great for you – great robber, great fibber, great loser.

The phunniest pharaoh phellers

The pharaohs ruled for almost 3,000 years so there were bound to be a few odd ones among all that lot. If there had been newspapers around in those days the headlines would have been horrible. If any had survived, they'd be a bit crumbly by now and key words would be missing. Can you replace them?

The following words fit the gaps: granny's hair, money, goose, murder, elephants, magician, lion, hippo, grandfather, Greek. But which goes where?

1 HORROR! IS TUTANKHAMUN VICTIM OF ____?

SHOCK! 2 TUTANKHAMUN'S WIDOW, PRINCESS ANKHESENAMUN, MARRIES — — !

3 ASTONISHING! TUTANKHAMUN BURIED WITH A LUMP OF HIS ——— !

Wonder! 4 HAIR CLIP FOUND BY ———!

AMAZING! PHARAOH'S 5 ENTERTAINER PUTS HEAD BACK ON — — !

SENSATION! HOR AHA IS 6 CARRIED OFF BY A —— !

ASTOUNDING! 7 KING RAMESSES II FACES ENEMY ARMY WITH JUST THE HELP OF A ____!

Wow! 8 Thutmose III escapes being killed by — — !

9 DEPLORABLE! PSAMMETICHUS HOLDS OFF SCYTHIAN INVASION WITH MASS OF —— !

EGYPTIAN SHAME! 10 QUEEN CLEOPATRA IS A ——— .

Answers:

1 murder – some people believe the young Pharaoh was murdered by his own uncle, Ay, who went on to take the throne. But in 2005 the mummy was given an x-ray. Tutankhamun's leg was broken and that is probably what led to his death. Murder is a better story.

2 grandfather – When Ay saw Tutankhamun die he decided the best way to get the throne was to marry his widow, Ankhesenamun. She tried to run off with a foreign prince but that didn't work. In the end she was forced to marry her grandad.

3 granny's hair – Tutankhamun was buried with a lump of his granny's hair in his coffin. No one knows why, but maybe he was fond of his mummy's mummy.

4 magician – Pharaoh Sneferu's wife lost her hair clip in a lake as she rowed across it. Sneferu ordered his court magician to find it. It was reported that the magician folded the lake in half and walked across to the clip. Oh, yeah? And there are fairies at the bottom on my garden.

5 goose – the pharaohs had all sorts of court entertainers. The one who appeared to remove the heads of geese and put them back on was obviously a clever trickster. But could he do anything with your Christmas turkey?

6 hippo – Pharaoh Hor Aha died when he was carried off by a hippopotamus. This probably served him right because he was out hippo hunting at the time. It was kill or be killed for the hippo.

7 lion – Ramesses faced the Hittite army with just his pet lion as backup. Then his friends turned up and attacked the Hittites from behind. Ramesses (and the lion) were saved.

8 elephants – Thutmose III was a great Pharaoh who defeated all Egypt's enemies. But he had a few close shaves with death along the way. In Syria he was almost trampled to death by a herd of wild elephants.

9 money – By 630 BC Egypt was past its best. Enemies weren't defeated, they were bribed. And – big mistake – the Greeks were paid to come to Egypt to help with the fighting. A bit like inviting a fox into your hen house.

10 Greek – Cleopatra is probably the most famous Egyptian queen … except she wasn't an Egyptian queen. She ruled after Egypt was conquered by the Greeks. She was the seventh queen of that name.

Potty pyramids

The pyramids were built as tombs for the pharaohs after they left this life. They were H-U-G-E and were filled with goodies so the kings would be as rich in the next life as they had been in this life.

History teachers have been telling us about Ancient Egypt and its pyramids since, well, since the days of Ancient Egypt. But there are some 'facts' they may have got wrong. Here are a few you might have heard…

1. Pyramid pain

Each one of the great pyramids took 100,000 slaves twenty years to build.

Who said that? A Greek visitor, called Herodotus. Old H was the world's first historian and a bit of a storyteller. You can't believe everything he said.

In ancient times he had TWO names…

When it came to facts about Egypt he was 'Herodotus – the father of mistakes'.

He asked the Egyptians…

Herodotus's mistake was to BELIEVE them! The Egyptians were just showing off.

The *Horrible Histories* truth is…

- Each pyramid was built by around 25,000 men.
- The pharaoh did not have 100,000 slaves in the whole of Egypt.
- They were free men, not slaves – they even went on strike when their pay was late.
- They were well fed with beef and ale – there was a fish factory and a bakery to keep them fed.
- They probably took just five years to build one pyramid.

But historians believed Herodotus and copied his mistake in their books. The mistake was repeated for thousands of years. Some school books today STILL give Herodotus' version of events.

2. Silly slopes

Some history books say: 'The Egyptians built a ramp up the side of the pyramid so they could drag the stones up to the top.'

The trouble is that a ramp of clay, mud, stones and bricks would crumble when a 16-tonne stone was dragged up it.

And another teeny problem is that the ramp would have to be many miles long … and it would take longer to build than the pyramid.

Other history books say the Egyptians may have built a ramp that went round the growing pyramid like a corkscrew. But that takes just as much building and is just as crumbly.

The *Horrible Histories* truth is … nobody really knows how the pyramids were built.

In the 1980s a British builder came up with a clever suggestion: maybe the Egyptians used wooden jacks that lifted the blocks up one step at a time. Teams of men could work very quickly. They could finish the whole job in thirteen years and it would cost about £300 million in today's money.

It's a clever idea, and it could work, but remember the *Horrible Histories* truth … nobody really knows.

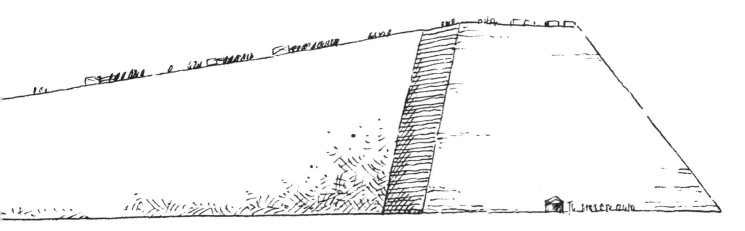

3. Pyramidiots

Some history books will tell you that the Egyptians were great at maths – even better than your teacher.

Here's why they think the Egyptians were such brainy boffins…

People who believe the pyramids have magical secrets are called 'pyramidologists'. They started investigating the pyramids in the 1850s and modern pyramidologists are still selling millions of books around the world.

The *Horrible Histories* truth is … they are pyramidiots. The pyramids don't measure 365.242 sacred cubits. The pyramidiots didn't check their facts – they are as potty as the people who say…

4. Boney's battering

Some history books say that near the great pyramids at Giza the Egyptians built a massive stone monster. It is 72 metres long and 20 metres tall. It has the body of a lion and the head of a man. The Greek name for it is 'The Sphinx'.

These books go on to explain that a French army, led by Napoleon Bonaparte, landed in Egypt in 1798. The French took one look at the great ugly face and decided to use it for target practice. They blasted off its nose.

No, it's not funny having your nose picked on.

The *Horrible Histories* truth is … the French army did NOT destroy the sphinx's face. It was wrecked 500 years before they arrived. A report said:

In 1318 the Arab tribes were led by Mohammed Sa'im al-Dahr – he caused terrible injuries to the head of the Sphinx. Then, in the 1700s Mamaluk soldiers from Egypt turned their guns on the statue.

In 1737 the artist Frederick Norden drew pictures of the Sphinx with no nose – over 30 years before Napoleon Bonaparte was born.

So don't blame Boney.

Quick quiz

The word 'sphinx' means…?

a) mangler?

b) strangler?

c) stranger?

Answer: b) 'Strangler' was the name given by the Greeks to a creature that had the head of a woman, the body of a lion and the wings of a bird.

In Egypt, there are quite a few sphinxes, usually with the head of a king wearing a head-dress and the body of a lion. There are also sphinxes with ram's heads.

The famous Great Sphinx at Giza, the one with no nose, was probably carved around 2500 BC. Its face may have been the face of the Pharaoh Khafre.

Did you know…?

It wasn't only tourists who thought the Sphinx was a mighty mystery. The Ancient Egyptians worshipped it as a god.

Egyptian Prince Tuthmosis IV even saw the Sphinx in a dream. In 1400 BC he was having a nap between the Sphinx's paws. He dreamed that the Sphinx begged him to rescue it from the Sahara sands that were swallowing it.

Tuthmosis said the Sphinx spoke to him in the dream…

40

Did Tuthmosis dig his dad out of the sand? Of course he did.

The pyramids time forgot

Egypt has about one hundred pyramids.

But in Sudan, the country next door to Egypt, there are three times as many.

In ancient times the land was known as Kush. In 1650 BC the chieftains from Kush attacked Egypt. Their king was captured, killed and dangled from the mast of his own boat.

But the Kush were back in Egypt again in 770 BC and this time they beat the Egyptians in battle and ruled the country for the next hundred years. Then they went back home to Kush and kept on building pyramids long after the Egyptians had stopped.

The Kush also had some nasty habits – like human sacrifice. When a king in Kush died his ministers would…

① GATHER SIX WIVES AND SIX SLAVES OR PRISONERS OF WAR

② MARCH THEM TO THE TEMPLE

③ LINE THEM UP AND SMASH THEM OVER THE HEAD

④ LAY THE CORPSES OUT IN NEAT ROWS IN THE PYRAMID

Weird or what? The wives and slaves were supposed to serve the Kush king in the next life.

Just so he wouldn't get lonely they also killed dogs, camels and horses to bury with him.

There are 24 horses buried near the pyramids of Kurru in present-day Sudan. These were probably the horses that pulled the royal chariots. When King Piye[6] died they were killed so they could pull his chariots in the afterlife, as he soared through the heavens.

6 Say the word Piye like 'pie'. Many of his people kept sheep so he was really the first ever shepherds' Piye.

It's a rotten thing to do to the harmless horses. But King Piye loved horses.

There is a stone in Piye's tomb with a carved story. It shows Piye marching into a town he had just conquered. He found that the horses there were being badly treated and said…

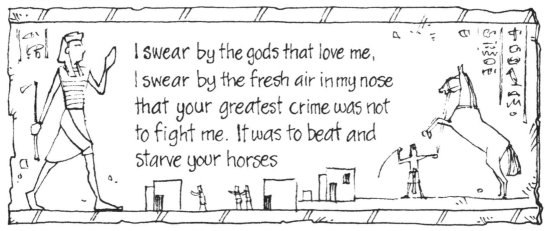

Anyway, it was believed that the ghosts of Kush kings all had wings – they could fly through the afterlife like a great bird. They didn't need dead horses to pull the chariots.

The deadly domes

Some of the biggest Kush mysteries lie in the dome tombs. These were huge mounds of earth made before the Kush had pyramids.

In the heart of the dome was a long corridor. It led to the king, who lay on a golden bed surrounded by his treasure.

There were also side passages all the way along that main corridor. And in every side passage there were dead men – lined up head to toe.

These passages were discovered in 1913. Historians said…

Wrong!

Modern tests have shown that most of the corpses belonged to the king's relations. This is a bit like your grandad dying and you being killed and buried with him. So what were they doing there?

And there's another mystery. How did they die? There are no marks on the skeletons that show they had been brutally battered.

Possibly. But the question is, did they drink the poison themselves – suicide? Or was it forced down them – murder?

Did you know…?

In the Kush city of Musawwarat the temple has huge ramps and corridors. The walls are carved with pictures of elephants.

Why did they need such huge passageways? To march elephants along, of course. This temple could have been where they trained their fighting elephants. It must have been a bit like driving a tank.

They then sold them to the Egyptians to use in wars.

Mad mummies

The Ancient Egyptians believed that one day the world would end. When this happened, they thought that everyone who had a body would move on to a wonderful afterlife. But if your body rotted away, you couldn't live in the afterlife. The Egyptians felt it was their duty to make sure that their dead pharaohs didn't rot. So they turned them into mummies.

A. Rip open the front of the body and take out the liver, the stomach, the intestines and the lungs – but leave the heart inside

B. Throw the brain away and pack the skull with 'natron' a sort of salt that stops bodies rotting

C. Stuff the empty body with rags to give it the right shape, then sew it up

D. Take the body to the 'beautiful house' – that's an open-ended tent in the fresh air so the disgusting smell is blown away

E. Wash the liver, the stomach, the intestines and lungs in wine and place them in their own sealed containers – canopic jars

Could YOU make a mummy? Below is an explanation of how to mummify a body. Unfortunately the instructions have been scrambled by a mummy's curse. Can you rearrange them?

(*Horrible Histories* note: If you get this completely right then you are an expert mummifier – or 'embalmer' as they were known. You can go out and practise on a favourite dead teacher if you like!)

Did you get them right? Now...

Make a mask that looks like the Pharaoh when he was alive and cover it with gold. Pop him in a stone coffin, stick him in his pyramid and have a party.

Everyone's invited – except the mummy of course.

Mummy makers

Some history books say that the Egyptians were experts at making mummies from the time of the very first pharaohs.

The *Horrible Histories* truth is ... it took them 1,500 years to become experts. In the meantime they made some horribly disgusting mistakes. The first mummies were just wrapped in bandages and they turned rotten...

Who taught the undertakers to make a better mummy? The cooks! They knew how to stop a dead animal going rotten – throw away the insides and cover the rest in salt.

The messy mummifiers then found that the fingernails and toenails dropped off after the salt had shrunk the hands and feet, so they learned to tie them on with thread.

Some clumsy undertakers found the dried-out bodies went as brittle as a twig and bits snapped off them.

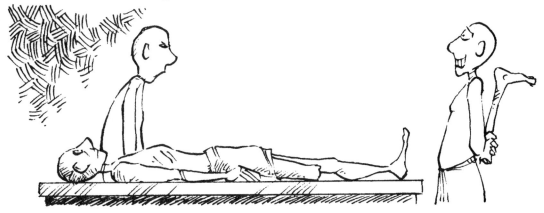

To solve the problem they rubbed oil into the dried-out corpse.

The gutted kings were stuffed with linen – but sometimes the embalmers used a bag of sawdust or moss. The arms, legs and face still looked skinny and ugly and that was no way to travel to the afterlife. So the mummifiers...

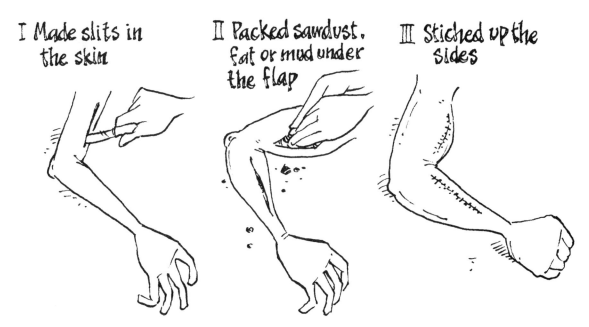

I Made slits in the skin

II Packed sawdust, fat or mud under the flap

III Stiched up the sides

But some clumsy undertakers tried to pack in too much and the corpse burst open.

Messy!

And you thought the Egyptians were experts?

Mummy magic

Of course desert-dry Egyptian summers dry up and preserve bodies anyway. An ancient peasant was buried in the desert sands and his body dried up but didn't rot. He's in the British Museum today and the keepers have given him a nickname. Here's how to work out what it is...

The following mummies will tell you a bit of mummy magic. But some of them aren't telling the truth. Take the liars away and the ones that are left will spell out the peasant's nickname.

EYES WERE ALWAYS LEFT IN MUMMIES

IF A BIT FALLS OFF MY BODY, EMBALMERS WILL REPLACE IT WITH A LUMP OF WOOD

THE LAST MUMMY WAS MADE IN 55 BC

PEOPLE IN BRITAIN WATCHED MUMMIES BEING UNWRAPPED FOR FUN

I WAS BURIED WITH A SCROLL OF MAGIC SPELLS CALLED 'THE BOOK OF THE DEAD'

51

Answer: G-I-N-G-E-R

Here's why…

Y – No. Sometimes eyes were replaced with black stones, though Ramesses IV was given two little onions! They'd be pickled onions if they were soaked in natron. Imagine eating those with your chips.

G – Yes. Bits often fell off bodies – or maybe a passing jackal nicked a few fingers! Embalmers would replace the missing bits with a ball of linen or a piece of wood.

I – Yes. In Victorian times people flocked to Dr Pettigrew's unwrappings. They were a sell-out like today's pop concerts. On one occasion the Archbishop of Canterbury was turned away because the hall was full.

O – No. Dr Pettigrew's work was so popular that the Duke of Hamilton asked to be mummified – after his death, of course. Pettigrew mummified him in 1852 and the daft duke was buried in a stone coffin – like a pharaoh.

N – Yes. The spells were there to protect the mummy in its dangerous journey to the afterlife.

52

U – No. The 'Books of the Dead' were prayers of protection against evil spirits NOT curses. The 'Mummy's Curse' idea is nineteenth-century nonsense and twentieth-century tosh!

T – No. Once a person reaches the afterlife his heart will be weighed on a set of scales. If the heart is heavy with wickedness then he will be eaten by 'the Devourer' – a monster that is part crocodile, part hippopotamus and part lion.

G – Yes. Mummies, the Egyptians said, had boiling lakes and rivers of fire to cross before they reached the afterlife. There was also a snake that spat poison at them. The mummies needed their 'Book of the Dead' as a magic charm to ward off evil.

E – Yes. A thousand years after they were buried, some mummies were dug up and used as magical healing potions. A mummy could be ground into a powder. King Charles II of England sprinkled powdered mummy over himself to get some mummy greatness! Yeuch!

H – No. The Victorians bought and sold bits of mummy to decorate their houses! A mummy foot or hand in a glass case was quite common.

R – Yes. Dug-up mummies became so common 200 years ago that they were thrown into ovens. In the famous pharaohs' graveyard known as the Valley of the Kings (by the Nile), mummies were used as fuel so the poor people could eat.

You should end up with the word 'Ginger' – the mummy's nickname. The museum keepers called him that because he had red-brown hair.

But … there is a story that 'Ginger' wasn't an Ancient Egyptian mummy after all. The British Museum collectors were tricked. They went to Egypt looking for mummies and a crooked dealer sold the Brits a fairly new corpse that he'd dried out!

There is even a story that the dealer sold them the corpse of his own brother!

Super sacrifices

The Egyptians believed everyone was made up of two parts – the body and the spirit. They called the spirit 'Ka'.

Your body might die but your Ka could live on … if it had somewhere to live.

The best place for the Ka to live after death was in the person's dead body – and that's why bodies were mummified.

Even after death, the Ka could get hungry so people were buried with food and drink.

The gods worshipped by the Egyptians were Kas, and they lived in statues. But, just like humans, Ka corpses had to be fed. A mummy had to have its mouth opened so it could eat.

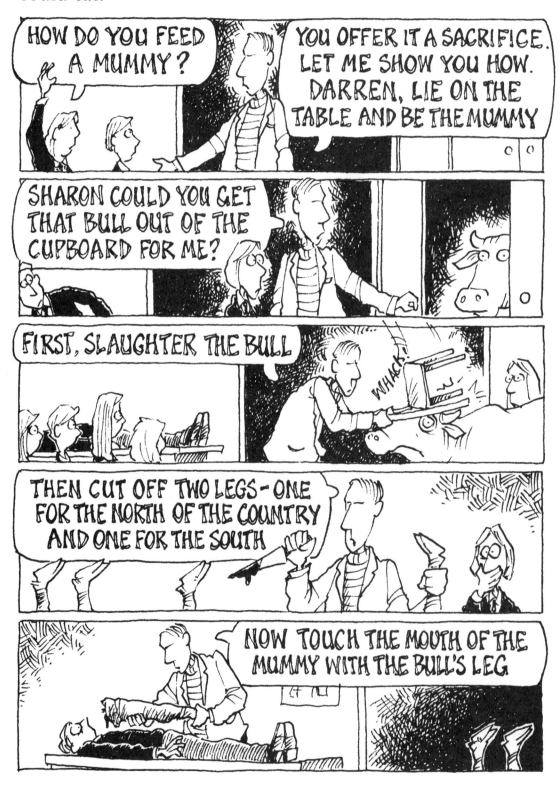

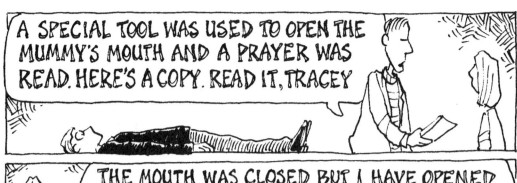

A SPECIAL TOOL WAS USED TO OPEN THE MUMMY'S MOUTH AND A PRAYER WAS READ. HERE'S A COPY. READ IT, TRACEY

THE MOUTH WAS CLOSED BUT I HAVE OPENED YOUR MOUTH AND TEETH, YOUR EYES WERE CLOSED BUT I HAVE OPENED THEM. I HAVE OPENED YOUR MOUTH WITH THE IRON TOOL THAT ANUBIS USED. THE DEAD WILL WALK AND TALK. HIS BODY WILL JOIN THE GODS IN THEIR HOUSE. HE SHALL BE GIVEN A CROWN BY HORUS

THEY FINISHED OFF BY SAYING, "YOU ARE YOUNG AGAIN, YOU SHALL LIVE AGAIN FOREVER"

...WISH HE'D TRY THAT ON ME

Mad mummies quiz

Don't wrap your mummy till you've tried this quick quiz. See how much you know before you begin binding with bandages. Score 10 and you are bound to be good.

1 The Arabs were the first to uncover ancient mummies. They thought the bodies were wrapped in something they called 'mumiya' – a sticky black stuff that goes hard. What would we call this stuff?
a) Bandages b) Tar
c) Toffee

2 When was the famous mummy of Tutankhamun dug up?
a) 1822 b) 1872 c) 1922

3 Some time between 1352 and 1336 BC King Akhenaten argued with his daughter and sent her for execution. What spiteful thing did he have done to the corpse?
a) Cut off its hair so no one would admire her beauty any more.
b) Cut off a hand so she couldn't go into the afterlife.
c) Cut off its finger to get a ring back.

4 What was the punishment for grave-robbing in Ancient Egypt?
a) Horrible torture
b) Horrible execution
c) Horrible torture followed by horrible execution

5 A grave robber reached into a coffin to steal some gold. The lid of the coffin fell and trapped him, then the roof of the tomb collapsed and killed him. He was found later, his skeleton hand still trapped in the coffin. How many years was his corpse there?

a) 26 years b) 260 years c) 2,600 years

6 A pharaoh's mother could be given a rich burial, too. The mother of Cheops had a burial shaft dug so deep that no one could rob her coffin. Yet they did. How?

a) They dug a tunnel through the rock to reach the coffin.

b) They hijacked the coffin on its way to the burial shaft.

c) They pinched the valuables before she was buried.

7 An 1880s tomb robber, Mohammed, was caught after selling the tomb treasures of 30 mummies. What did the Egyptians do with Mohammed?

a) They gave him a reward for finding the mummies.

b) They cut off his hands.

c) They cut off his head.

8 Archaeologists learn a lot from mummies. What do they learn from mummy teeth?

a) The ancient Egyptians used toothpaste.

b) The ancient Egyptians ate beef burgers.

c) Egyptian bread was coarse and gritty.

Answers:

1b) 'Mumiya' was the Arab word for tar. Of course the Arabs were wrong – it wasn't tar – but the name 'mumiya' has stuck … like tar!

2c) It was found by the archaeologist Howard Carter in a burial chamber (not a pyramid). Carter was sponsored by Lord Carnarvon and Carnarvon died six months later – and that started the rumour of the mummy's curse!

3b) Only a complete body could pass into the afterlife so the cruel king was trying to prevent her enjoying Egyptian heaven! There is a story that the mummified hand was taken to England in the 1920s – and the girl's ghost haunted its owners.

4c) But this didn't stop the robbers. Their favourite trick was to bribe the tomb-makers and the guards to make the robbery easier. Sometimes the pharaoh's own priests helped in the robbery.

5a) The robber was trapped in the tomb and his greedy skeleton was found by archaeologists in 1970. They knew when he had died because in the skeleton's tattered coat was a newspaper – dated 1944.

6c) Modern archaeologists dug up the coffin of Cheops' mother, Hetepheres. It had not been disturbed, yet there were just two poor silver bracelets with the skeleton. Where was the fabulous treasure Cheops said he'd buried with her? It was nicked before the coffin was sealed. Khufu's prime minister, Yussef, is the chief suspect.

7a) Mohammed was rewarded for finding the mummies – which he hadn't touched. The Egyptian government 'forgot' about the loot he'd stolen and gave him a job … as a guide, showing tourists round the tombs.

8c) The teeth are usually badly worn down from eating bread. The corn was ground between stones and grit from the stones got into the flour. Eating bread must have been like eating sandpaper. Yeuch!

Did you know…?

Pharaohs were buried with mummies of animals. Cats were popular but they also made mummies out of …

The truth about Tutankhamun

King Tutankhamun was dead as a duck's toenail and he was buried in a rock tomb.

Did he rest in peace?

Not for long. If the Ancient Egyptians had had ancient policemen then the report might have looked like this:

 VALLEY OF THE KINGS CONSTABULARY

Crime: Grave robbing	Date: 1327 BC

Address:	King Tutankhamun's Tomb, Valley of the Kings, Egypt

Report: I was called to the tomb of King T. at 6 a.m. As I was asleep at the time I was not amused, I can tell you. 'Another kid been eaten by a croc?' I groaned.

'No, sir,' Sergeant Paneb said. 'King Tutankhamun's grave's been robbed.

I sighed and turned over on the straw. 'That was yesterday, Sergeant,' I said. 'I looked into it. I looked into the case and I looked into the grave. The robbers had stolen bronze arrow-heads off the king's arrows, some fine materials and some perfume jars.'

'But sir,' Paneb tried to interrupt. He's always doing that.

'They were clever,' I told him. 'They only took things that could not be traced back to the tomb – I mean one arrow-head is pretty much like any other arrow-head ... unless it's in YOUR head, of course. They can do a bit of damage those arrow-heads.'

'But, sir –' he cut in. Did I mention he's always doing that?

'They tried to steal some golden furniture,' I went on. 'They thought they could melt it down. Then they found it was just wooden furniture covered in gold leaf. Hah! Threw it back in the tomb, didn't they?'

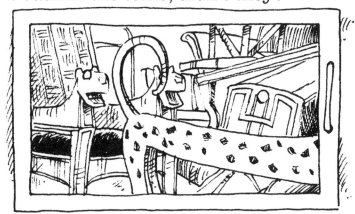

'But sir!' Paneb cried.

I shouted him down. 'The grave was sealed with tons of limestone chips. Grave closed, case closed,' I said and turned over to get some sleep.

'But, sir,' Paneb went on. 'They've robbed it again!'

'What? What?' I said and jumped off my straw bed. 'Why didn't you say so, you buffoon?'

'The robbers made a tunnel through the chippings and broke in again.'

'A tunnel? That must have taken them all night,' I said, looking for my tunic and sandals.

'Seven hours at least,' Paneb said. 'This time they got jewels out.'

'No clues?' I asked as I stumbled out into the morning air.

'Just this, sir,' Paneb said. He jangled a twisted scarf in front of me. When I opened it I found eight gold rings. 'I think they were in such a hurry to get away they dropped part of the loot.'

Eight rings – not much of a clue.

By the time I got to the grave the dead king's minister, Maya, was there. His face was like a stone statue. He glared at me. 'You are too late,' he snarled.

'It's never too late to catch a thief,' I told him brightly.

'It is,' he snapped. 'My guards caught them running away. You have failed.' He took a step towards me and poked me in the shoulder. I hate that. 'I will make Sergeant Paneb my new chief of police.'

'I'm out of a job?' I cried.

'Oh, no,' Maya said viciously. 'You have a new job – you can be the royal executioner. You can start with the grave robbers we caught.'

I groaned. Because we all know what happens to grave robbers, don't we?

Well? Do we?

The tomb of Tutankhamun WAS robbed twice shortly after his funeral. And a scarf, twisted round eight precious rings, WAS found in the tunnel that the robbers used.

We don't know if the ring robbers were caught or if they escaped. But we're pretty sure what would have happened to them if they had been caught. And it wasn't very nice.

If you were a pharaoh and someone was caught grave-robbing, what punishment would you give them?

a) Have them buried alive in the grave they tried to rob.

b) Have them sacrificed in the temple of Baba, the cannibal god.

c) Have them placed on a pole with a sharp end.

Answer: c) This is called impaling. But the victims weren't stabbed with the sharp pole. They were lowered on to it slowly. Their weight pressed down on the point – the more they struggled the further it tore into them. It was a slow and painful death.

You wouldn't want that to happen to you. But you wouldn't want to be the executioner either ... would you?

DUNNO, COULD BE PAYBACK FOR MAKING A MUMMY OF ME

The curse of Tutankhamun's tomb

Mummies are a bit creepy. Looking at corpses of long-dead people is enough to give you goosebumps on your goosebumps. But it's just not creepy enough for some people!

Some people like to imagine the mummies aren't just shrivelled flesh – they believe the mummy spirits wander around, putting curses on the living people who disturbed their rest and robbed their graves!

Tutankhamun's tomb was discovered in 1922 and started a wave of 'curse' rumours but *Horrible Histories* has found out the truth. Someone at some time has said all the following ten stories are true. Can you work out which stories are simple LIES (L), which are MISTAKES (M) and which are TRUE (T) but can be explained?

1 The Earl of Carnarvon paid for the expedition to dig up the mummy of Tutankhamun and he died within six months of the discovery. L or M or T?

2 When Tutankhamun's mummy was unwrapped the archaeologists found a curse wrapped in the bandages. It said: 'Those who enter this sacred tomb shall swiftly be visited by the wings of death.' L or M or T?

3 Lord Carnarvon's friend, Count Hamon, owned an ancient mummy's hand. It was as soft and fresh as the day it was cut off the mummy. L or M or T?

4 Lord Carnarvon pricked his cheek on a poisoned arrow-head in the tomb and died from the poison. L or M or T?

5 When Lord Carnarvon died his favourite dog howled at the exact moment of his death. The dog was 3,000 miles away in England. L or M or T?

6 Mohammed Ibrahim had been very much against moving Tutankhamun's treasures to France in 1966. He fought to keep the mummy in Egypt, but he lost the fight in a final meeting. Ibrahim left the meeting – and walked into the path of a taxi. He died instantly. L or M or T?

7 A worker in the British Museum was fastening labels to items stolen from Tutankhamun's tomb. He dropped dead. L or M or T?

8 Arthur Mace was one of the first people to enter the tomb and he died shortly afterwards. L or M or T?

9 American millionaire George Gould visited the tomb. He was fine before he went but died soon after. L or M or T?

10 The mummy's 'curse' is in fact Ancient Egyptian germs that were sealed into the tomb 3,000 years ago. L or M or T?

Answers:

1 **True, but** … Carnarvon was a sickly man. He'd been in a car accident a while before the mummy-discovery and was not fit for the heat of Egypt.

2 **Lies.** A newspaper reported this curse soon after Carnarvon's death. The mummies were buried with a 'Book of the Dead' in their coffins. Some people believe this book cursed grave robbers. The truth is that the 'Book of the Dead' was a collection of prayers and charms to protect the person's spirit in the next life. It was not a curse book.

3 **Lies.** Hamon did indeed own a mummy hand, but he made a lot of money as a fortune-teller. It suited him to tell stories about ghostly experiences.

4 **Mistake.** Lord Carnarvon got a mosquito bite on his face – not a poison-arrow scratch. He cut it open when he was shaving and that gave him blood poisoning and a fever. He was very weak and caught a lung infection. That's what killed him, not the scratch on the face.

5 **True, but** … this was just a creepy story told by Lord Carnarvon's son. But what has it to do with a mummy's curse? Another story said all the lights in Egypt's capital city Cairo went out at that moment. Again, creepy – but nothing to do with the 'curse'?

6 **True, but** … this was a 'friend' of the mummy trying to keep it in Egypt. Surely the curse wouldn't have affected him?

7 **Lies.** The British Museum never had any objects from Tut's tomb.

8 **True, but** … Mace had been ill before he entered the tomb. He had pleurisy and there was no cure for this illness in 1922.

9 **Mistake.** Gould was not in good health before his visit. He went to Egypt because he was ill and thought the warm weather would help. He did visit the tomb, but the stress of the travelling killed him.

10 **Mistake.** The air in the tomb wouldn't be very healthy, but King Tut's germs wouldn't kill a visitor today.

Did you know…?

In March 1923, a writer named Marie Corelli (real name Mary Mackay) wrote the following warning…

There will be terrible danger for anyone who enters the tomb of Tutankhamun!

What made mad Marie say that? Well, on the day Howard Carter opened the tomb, his pet canary was swallowed by a cobra, and cobras were the guards of the pharaohs!

Poor tweeter. But the canary hadn't gone into the tomb – Carter had. What happened to him?

a) He was swallowed by a cobra the next day.

b) He swallowed a cobra and lived another two days.

c) He lived another 17 years, dying just before his sixty-fifth birthday.

Answer: c) Not much of a curse!

Scotch missed bone

Don't go to No. 15 Learmonth Gardens in Edinburgh!

Oh, very well. Go there if you must. But beware the mummy's curse … I said, the mummy's curse.[7]

In 1936 Sir Alexander Hay Seton went to Egypt. He and his wife Zeyla visited a tomb. A guide led them down a stone staircase into an underground room.

'These are the bones of an ancient princess,' the guide said, and he showed A and Z a crumbling mummy.

When no one was looking Zeyla slipped a bit of bone from the mummy into her handbag. Was she potty about a patella or crazy for a cranium? No, she was batty for a bit of backbone.

She took it home to 15 Learmonth Gardens in Edinburgh and put it in a glass case[8]. Then the trouble started.

As Sir Alex left the house one day a piece of the roof crashed down and missed him by a whisker.

Furniture was broken. A table turned over in the night.

Sounds disturbed the sleep of the horrified Hay Setons.

Ornaments rose in the air and flew across the room.

---

7 There should be at lease ten exclamation marks here to add a bit of drama! I can't be bothered to type ten exclamation marks so I'll leave a space and you can add your own.

8 It is always best to put your stolen bones in a glass case. Especially if they are leg bones. The case stops them from running away. But this was a spine bone – a glass case was clearly a mistake because the bone was spyin' on them.

Worst of all, the ghostly figure of an Egyptian priest popped up from time to time. Visitors and servants all saw it.

A newspaper reporter heard about the curse and asked if he could borrow the bone.

Sir Alex sent the bone on loan (alone). The reporter came back two weeks later. 'Nothing happened,' he laughed. But a few days later he was desperately ill in hospital.

Sir Alex lost his money when business went wrong.

'It's the curse of the stolen bone!' Sir Alex moaned. 'Destroy it!' he ordered.

Zeyla would not hear of it.

Sir Alex was too lazy to destroy it himself (you could say he was bone idle) so he went to his cousin who was a monk. First the monk blessed it, then he destroyed it. The bone was burned to ashes in a stove.

Zeyla could not forgive Alex, so she left him.

Alex wrote…

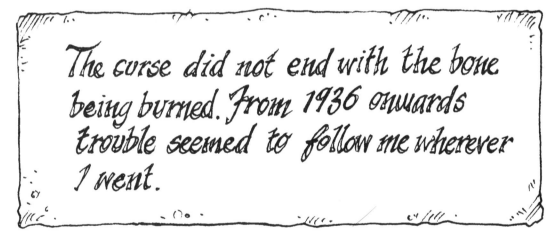

The curse did not end with the bone being burned. From 1936 onwards trouble seemed to follow me wherever I went.

He died in 1963 at the age of 58.

Misery for Menkaure

Pharaohs didn't just leave curses behind. Sometimes the pharaoh himself was cursed.

The gods told Menkaure that he would die in six years' time.

He decided to cheat the gods. Menkaure gave orders for candles to be burned after dark so, in his palace, there was never any day or night. The Pharaoh lived day AND night, so he said he lived twelve years – not six.

Then he died.

But WHY was he cursed?

a) He was too cruel to the peasants.

b) He was too kind to the peasants.

c) He was too cruel to his granny.

Answer: b) Menkaure was not as harsh as the other pharaohs. That upset the gods who said he SHOULD have been. Bet the peasants were pleased.

Cruel crime time

Ancient Egypt was as full of crime as the Wild West in the USA or the dark streets of Victorian London.

And the crimes haven't changed much since the days of the pharaohs – murder, theft and cruelty. Times change – people don't.

Here are a few horribly historical crime stories from Ancient Egypt…

PLAN TO BAM RAM!

1151 BC – There was a plot to murder Ramesses III, hatched by one of his wives, Tiy. The plan was to attack Ramesses inside his palace while rebels started a revolt in the cities outside.

The plotters were caught and their sentence would have been death. But unusually the judges said…

YOU MUST TAKE YOUR OWN LIFE AND YOU MUST DO IT NOW, HERE IN THIS COURT

That must have made a right mess on the court floor.

LAW AND DISORDER

What do you do with a judge who breaks the law?

In the Ramesses trial a couple of the judges were caught having dinner with the plotters. It was their turn to be put on trial. The judges' judge said…

I SENTENCE YOU TO HAVE YOUR NOSE AND EARS SLICED OFF

One of the crooked judges killed himself before the executioner could carve him. The other had a bit of Egyptian plastic surgery…

I'LL NEVER HEAR ANOTHER CASE AGAIN

FAILED NILE MEANS NASTY NIBBLES

The Nile flooded every year and watered the crops. The farmers gathered the corn and it lasted them a year till the next flood.

But when the Nile failed to flood there was no food. What did they do?

Around 1900 BC there was a famine. The Egyptian Heqanakhte left his family in Thebes to go in search of food in the north. He wrote a letter home that told a foul famine tale…

Heqanakhte doesn't say if they were eating corpses or killing people. (Corpses can be old and chewy – much better to kill a nice fresh feller.)

GIVEN A GOOD HIDE-ING

In 1315 BC the Pharaoh Ay died … aye, die he did. Horemheb, an army general, seized power and passed laws to look after the poor.

He was worried that too many soldiers were stealing cattle-skins (hides) from the lower classes. So he made a new punishment for hide thieves…

STICK UP FOR THIEVES

Seti I had his laws carved into a cliff at Nauri. The gods in the temple owned cattle in the area. If you stole cattle from a god you had a really nasty punishment waiting for you – impaling.

Seti's law said…

PUNISHMENT FOR A CATTLE THIEF WILL BE CASTING HIM DOWN AND IMPALING HIM ON A STAKE. HIS WIFE AND CHILDREN WILL BECOME SLAVES

That means a sharp pole was placed into the ground. The thief was taken to a cliff and thrown down on to the point.

A sharp lesson.

Ruthless robbers

Great Egyptians were buried with great wealth. Poor Egyptians wanted it, so they robbed the graves. They stole the gold to melt it and sell it. They didn't mind what damage they did.

Of course all the graves have been robbed by now – some were robbed at the time of the burial and many were cleaned out by greedy treasure hunters in the nineteenth century.

The robbers said:

WE ARE COLLECTING HISTORICAL MATERIAL FOR YOUR EDUCATION

That's a bit like a bank robber saying…

MY HOBBY IS COLLECTING BANK NOTES

… they're all just robbers!

In 1901 a British historian, Flinders[9] Petrie, was 'exploring' Pharaoh Dojer's tomb. He found an arm wrapped in bandages stuffed into a crack in the wall. No one is sure how it got there.

Maybe an early robber had ripped it off and hidden it. Other grave robbers had not seen the arm – or the rich bracelets on the wrist.

One pharaoh went to amazing lengths to keep robbers away from his grave…

9 Cinders may be short for Cinderella. But Flinders is not short for Flinderella – just thought you'd like to know.

A-Maze-ing Amenemhet

Pharaoh Amenemhet was worried about his funeral…

But Amenemhet was worried about robbers stealing his body after it was buried. You don't have any fear of that, do you?

Amenemhet needed a plan to keep thieves away from his tomb. He believed that his burial room had to be filled with riches if he was to be comfortable in the afterlife. But he had learned his lesson from other dead pharaohs, who had ordered that the passages of their pyramids be plugged with massive granite blocks after the burial. Tomb robbers had simply cut through the softer limestone walls around them. They found the burial rooms and grabbed the treasures.

How could Amenemhet stop them?

Sadly machine guns hadn't been invented. No – he needed something so clever that no one would ever find their way in to the centre of the tomb.

He decided to build a pyramid where the passages inside were a maze. There would be secret sliding doors, false corridors, and hidden rooms.

No one but the Pharaoh himself knew all the secrets. The workmen who built the maze were led to their work each day with blindfolds on.

Since Amenemhet was the only one who knew the way through his amazing tomb, we should get him to tell us the route…

79

ONCE A THIEF HAS CARVED THROUGH THESE BLOCKS, HE WILL DISCOVER HE HAS BEEN TRICKED—THE PASSAGEWAY IS A DEAD END

THE RIGHT PATH IS A CORRIDOR CLOSED ONLY BY A WOODEN DOOR

THIS OPENS INTO ANOTHER DEAD-END PASSAGE

TO GET OUT OF THIS PASSAGE YOU HAVE TO FIND A HIDDEN SLIDING STONE

YOU FIND YOURSELF IN A BARE ROOM; FROM HERE A SECRET TRAPDOOR LEADS TO A LONG PASSAGEWAY FILLED IN WITH MASSIVE STONE BLOCKS

BREAK THROUGH THE BLOCKS AND FIND TWO OPEN BURIAL SHAFTS IN THE FLOOR. ONE IS FILLED IN BY STONE SLABS; THE OTHERS SEEM TO BE EMPTY

Now, the question is, did it work?
Was Amenemhet's tomb…
a) robbed in ancient times?
b) safe until the twentieth century?

Answer: a) Somehow, tomb robbers got through all these defences. They emptied the burial chamber but, angry at all the dead ends, they took a horrible revenge. They set fire to Amenemhet's mummy, ensuring that he would not live in the afterlife.

It seems as though grave robbers would stop at nothing to steal a pharaoh's treasures.

Loret's horror

In 1898 a French historian named Victor Loret explored the tomb of Amenhotep II. He hoped to find a coffin and a neatly wrapped mummy. Instead he found something out of a horror movie.

He described it in his diary…

- I had only a candle for light and almost stumbled into a well - a deep pit used to catch the water when the Valley of the Kings flooded.

- I placed a ladder over the ugly hole and crawled over to the other side. I was in a small room. Broken statues were scattered over the floor.

- Thieves had been there before me. A doorway led into another room. That was where I hoped to find the mummy.

- It was deep into the night and I was afraid. But I stepped through the door with my spluttering candle in my hand

- A horrible sight met my eyes. There was a small boat in the room - the boat built to carry the Pharaoh to the next world.

- But in place of the mummy there was a corpse, black and grinning. Its face was turned towards me. I felt it was staring at me.

- Its long, brown hair was in clumps around its head. I never dreamed I was looking at a mummy that had been torn from its wrapping.

- There was a hole in its chest and another in its skull. I thought I was looking at the victim of a human sacrifice

- Or was this a tomb robber who had been killed by the other robbers and left to rot alone down here?

- Was it, maybe, a thief who had been caught by the guards and killed on the spot? And still the eyes stared at me!

Loret had found the mummy of a prince. It had been unwrapped soon after it had been buried – the thieves had been looking for jewels wrapped in its bandages.

Loret's shocks were not over, though. He found three other exposed mummies in the other rooms – a man, a woman and a boy.

The male mummy was King Amenhotep II. Some of the padding had been torn from its mouth in the search for jewels. A strip of cloth hung out like a dead tongue.

There were nine more coffins in the tomb. These contained nine wrecked mummies, which had been collected by King Pinedjem I in ancient times.

But thieves had got at them a second time.

Would YOU unwrap a corpse and smash open its body to steal its jewels?

Did you know ....?

You shouldn't feel too sorry for Amenhotep II. When he was alive he was pretty ruthless. In his 1425 BC battles against the Nubians he captured seven enemy princes and wanted them killed as sacrifices to the gods. Normally that job would have been given to an executioner. Amenhotep II killed them himself.

Rotten religion

The Egyptians told many stories about their gods. The trouble with Egyptian gods is that they all got a bit mixed up. Their stories were repeated for 3,000 years and they changed over time.

The sun god, Re, became mixed up with Amun (the god of the city of Thebes) and by around 1500 BC he had become one god – Amun-Re.

And the moon god Thoth sometimes appears as an ibis bird and sometimes as a baboon!

Great gods

There were two sorts of gods in Egypt – the great gods that looked after the whole country … and the little gods that looked after your house and family.

The great gods had temples and were fed with fat, fleshy sacrifices. The little gods didn't get so much as a stale bag of crisps. (Probably because crisps hadn't been invented.)

Here are some of the groovy gods you could have prayed to in Ancient Egypt.

1. AMUN (sometimes called Amoun or Amun-Ra)
Looks like … an ape, or a man with the head of a frog.
Worship him because … he's the top man, 'the king of the gods'.

HIS NICKNAME WAS THE GREAT HONKER BECAUSE HE HONKED LIKE A GOOSE

2. ANUBIS

Looks like … a man with the head of a jackal (or a dog).

Worship him because … he's the main mummy man.

HE WRAPPED UP BITS OF THE DEAD OSIRIS AND BROUGHT HIM BACK TO LIFE - A USEFUL TRICK - ANUBIS IS A GOOD GOD TO KNOW

3. HATHOR

Looks like … a woman with the ears of a cow, or a cow or a woman with horns and a sun disc on her head.

Worship her because … she's the goddess of music, dance and booze.

SHE IS A USEFUL GODDESS FOR KEEPING YOUR GRASS SHORT. COW… GRAZING… GEDDIT? OH NEVER MIND YOU PROBABLY DON'T WANT A DANCING COW ON YOUR LAWN ANYWAY

4. HORUS

Looks like … a hawk or a man with the head of a falcon.

Worship him because … he looks after children and the pharaoh – and he can cure snake bites.

HE'S UP THERE IN THE SKY LOOKING AFTER YOUR PHARAOH

5. ISIS

Looks … similar to Hathor. Often shown with horns and sun disc.

Worship her because … she's Horus's Mum.

> HER WINGS BREATHE LIFE INTO THE DEAD

6. KHEPRI

Looks like … a scarab or dung beetle.

Worship him because … he's the new-born sun god. He rolls the sun across the sky each day like a dung beetle rolls a ball of poo.

> DUNG BEETLES OFTEN POP OUT OF THE POO THEY'VE BEEN SLEEPING IN. THE EGYPTIANS THOUGHT THEY HAD HATCHED OUT OF NOTHING, SO KHEPRI WAS A GOD WHO CREATED HIMSELF

7. KHNUM

Looks like … a man with the head of a ram.

Worship him because … he's the god of the Nile and the pots that are made from its mud. He made people on his potter's wheel.

> WE'RE ALL HERE THANKS TO THIS MUDDY, MODELLING GOD

OSIRIS

Looks like … a man chopped into pieces then joined together again and wrapped in white linen like a mummy. His skin is green. He carries a shepherd's crook and a flail to make corn into flour.

Worship him because … he's another top god.

> HE WILL LOOK AFTER YOU WHEN YOU DIE

9. SETH

Looks like … a man with the head of a strange beast. Enough to give you nightmares.

Worship him because … he's the nasty brother of Osiris and son of Nut.[10] God of trouble.

> HE CHOPPED OSIRIS UP INTO BITS

10. THOTH

Looks like … one of three shapes – a baboon or an ibis bird or a man with an ibis's head. (Never as a man with a baboon's head. If you see one of those it's probably a history teacher.)

Worship him because … he's the god of writing and wisdom.

> WORSHIP HIM BECAUSE THEN YOU WILL DO WELL IN SCHOOL AND WHEN YOU DIE HE'S THE GOD WHO RECORDS THE WEIGHT OF YOUR HEART. A GOOD HEART WILL GET YOU INTO HEAVEN

10 No, no, no! Not the son of a nut. The son of Nut – goddess of the sky. Maybe she should have given savage Seth a crack round the ear when he was a kid. A sort of Nut cracker.

Horus horror

The god Horus had two eyes. Nothing new there then. But along came savage Uncle Seth and ripped out his left eye. He then tore the eye to pieces.

Horus FOUND the pieces of his left eye and popped them back in. But it was never as strong as his right eye.

Horus let his eyes float over the Earth to light it. The sun is the strong right eye, the Moon is his weak left eye.

Temple brain-teaser

Enter the Temple of Mystery. Can you match the right god to the gruesome stories?

If you can then *Horrible Histories* will award you a special prize –

WIN A TRIP -TO- EGYPT

FOR ONE LUCKY READER AND THEIR FAMILY
SIMPLY ANSWER TEN *EASY* QUESTIONS
SEND YOUR ENTRY WITH A £100 NOTE TO:
'The Great Terry Deary Egypt Scam, Cairo'

Small print. Please note, this offer applies only to readers over the age of 90 who are dead and mummified. Normal terms and conditions apply.

Even smaller print. Winners must be accompanied on the trip by their parents and pay for their own travel, meals and accommodation.

The middle column will give you a clue — as if an awesome Egyptian expert like you needs them!

Name	Clue	Story

1. Ammit — lion front and hippo bum

Munch!

A. Murders humans and feasts on their guts

2. Duamutef — head of jackal, body of man

Gutsy!

B. Looks after lungs of mummy

3. Hapy — baboon head, body of man

Chesty!

C. Sneezed and his snot became the gods

4. Nut — a cow

Gulp!

D. Known as 'She who Loves Silence'

5. Mafdet — a pan-ther

Ssss!

E. Was a dung beetle that rolled its eggs into a ball of animal

6. Meretseger – cobra shape

Shhh!

F. Looks after intestines of mummy

7. Baba – baboon

Dangerous!

G. Guards you against snake bites

8. Atum – man with a crown

Atchoo!

H. Eats evil hearts on judgement day

9. Sekhmet – a lioness

Guzzle!

I. Started to massacre all humans until she got too drunk

10. Khepri – god of the sun

Pooh!

J. Swallows the sun every night

Did you know…?

A peasant like you could become a god/dess. Gods were usually dead kings, but ordinary people could become gods too if they died in a certain way. How did they have to die?

a) By falling off a pyramid

b) Dying in battle saving a pharaoh

c) By drowning in the Nile

Answer: c) The River Nile was the most important thing in Egypt. Without its flooding there would just be a desert and no great nation. So the river became holy. And from around 1550 BC anyone who drowned in the River Nile could become a god and have their own little temple! So, you want to become an Egyptian god? Go take a long walk off a short plank over the Nile!

Killing ... and curing

It can be horrible if you are ill. But sometimes the cure is worse than the illness.

Which would you rather have? The pain of toothache … or the pain of a drill whizzing round your mouth?

But you are lucky. Lucky you weren't an Egyptian. If you had a broken bone then the doctor would mix a paste and slap it on…

The cure for a broken nose was to…

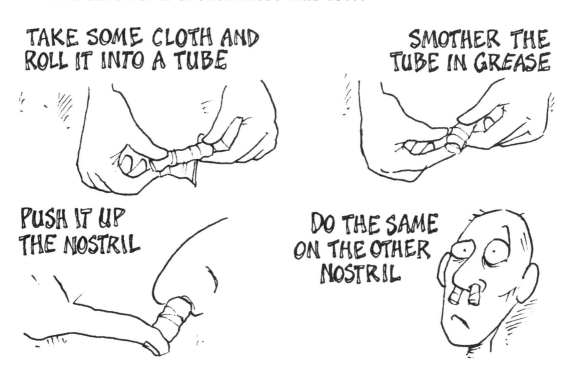

TAKE SOME CLOTH AND ROLL IT INTO A TUBE

SMOTHER THE TUBE IN GREASE

PUSH IT UP THE NOSTRIL

DO THE SAME ON THE OTHER NOSTRIL

Nice.

But these weren't the only disgusting cures.

Is your teacher going bald? Then offer him a mixture of viper's oil mixed with bats' ears[11]. Crush them all together and slap them on the bald patch.

The Egyptian cure for toothache is so disgusting I can't even tell you what it was!

What? You REALLY want to know? Oh, very well…

---

11 Or maybe not. Bats are protected species … and I haven't a clue what 'viper's oil' is.

Horrible Histories warning:
Do NOT read this if you are under the age of 75, suffer from nightmares, or faint at the thought of blood.

The cure was written down by the Greek visitor to Egypt, Hippocrates. But he was a bit odd. He thought you could make toothpaste by crushing three mice in the head of a hare.

One book for Egyptian doctors describes how to deal with a nasty cut...

Did you know...?
The Egyptians were sure that all illness was a result of what you ate. So they liked to diet and take herbs that would make all the poo run out of them for three days – sort of a clear-out. The servant who looked after the pharaoh's 'clear out' was known as the 'Shepherd of the Royal Backside'.

The 'Doctor! Doctor!' quiz

Could you become an Egyptian doctor? Here's a test to see if you're a medical mastermind…

The Egyptian doctors treated people with a mixture of medicine and magic. Some may have cured but others probably killed. Look at some of the Egyptian beliefs about death and doctoring and make up your own mind.

1 In England in the 1920s people were still using an Ancient Egyptian cure for children who wet the bed. What did the child have to eat?
a) A cooked mouse
b) A cooked louse
c) A crooked house

2 The Egyptians had a cure for night-blindness that modern doctors think may have worked. What did the Egyptians drink?
a) Blood from a white cat's tail
b) Juice from an ox's liver
c) Pee from a greyhound

3 The Egyptians used clever cures like onion juice (an antibiotic) and some horrible ones. In some medical scrolls the Egyptians describe how to make medicine using 19 different types of what?
a) Pee
b) Poo
c) Plum

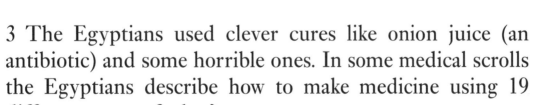

4 The Egyptian cure for a burn was to cover it in a stuff that really worked. What?
a) Jam b) Honey c) Money

Woeful Workers

Have parents and teachers ever told you to work hard at school? What do they say?

Some schools used to say…

Parents may threaten…

But the oldest threat is…

In fact this threat is so old that the Ancient Egyptians used it to bully their children. A man called Dua-Khety wrote down these threats for his son Pepi around 2000 BC. He makes life in Egypt sound horrible. Here is the top ten of terrible tradesmen…

12 This is an odd thing to say. How does the father know what fish poo smells like? Do YOU know what fish poo smells like? Where would you get the fish poo to find out? Where would you find a fish toilet?

THE MESSENGER FACES DANGERS ON THE ROAD – HE MIGHT BE TORN APART BY LIONS OR BEATEN BY ROBBERS

THE FURNACE-WORKER HAS SORE RED EYES AND HANDS THAT SMELL LIKE A CORPSE

THE WASHER-MAN WORKS AT THE RIVER AND IS IN DANGER FROM CROCODILES. HE EATS FOOD THAT IS MIXED WITH FILTH

THE FISHERMAN FALLS IN THE RIVER, WHERE HE MAY BE CRUSHED IN THE JAWS OF A HIPPO

So you see, the message is…

WORK HARD AT SCHOOL OR YOU MAY END UP WITH A TERRIBLE JOB

LIKE TEACHING

Did you know….?

Some history books say that the Ancient Egyptians had camels to do all their work. In 2000 BC the pharaoh gave camels to Abraham as a gift.

YES! IT SAYS SO IN THE BIBLE - GENESIS, CHAPTER 12, VERSE 16

The *Horrible Histories* truth is… they didn't. No one tamed a camel till around 1000 BC.

Super Scribes

The best job in Ancient Egypt was being a scribe – their job was to write. The scribe was his own boss, made lots of money and paid no taxes! What a life!

Trainee scribes spent seven years in scribe school, copying teacher's writing the way you copy off a whiteboard.

These young scribes would…

• Make their own pens by chewing the end of a reed to create a sort of paintbrush

• Carry a few different sizes of paintbrush-pens by sticking them behind their ears

• Use 'ink' that was actually a block of soot and gum (for black ink) or red soil for red ink. They would use the blocks of ink the way a modern painter uses watercolours.

So – got your reed? Chewed the end? Then you're ready to begin your training.

Here are a few foul Egyptian facts for you to copy – but first you have to fill in the missing words.

Missing words: statue, book, pig, severed hand, bag of corn, leopard, wooden beard, lettuce, woman, barrel of beer.

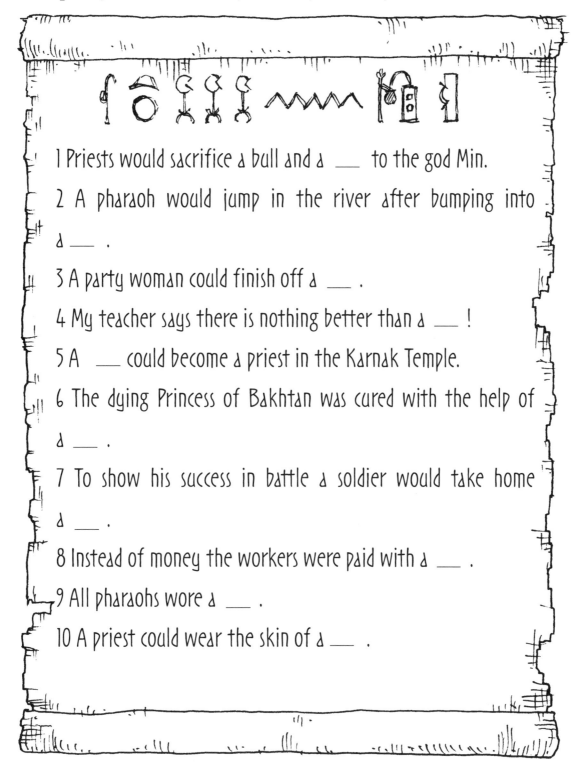

1 Priests would sacrifice a bull and a ___ to the god Min.

2 A pharaoh would jump in the river after bumping into a ___ .

3 A party woman could finish off a ___ .

4 My teacher says there is nothing better than a ___ !

5 A ___ could become a priest in the Karnak Temple.

6 The dying Princess of Bakhtan was cured with the help of a ___ .

7 To show his success in battle a soldier would take home a ___ .

8 Instead of money the workers were paid with a ___ .

9 All pharaohs wore a ___ .

10 A priest could wear the skin of a ___ .

Answers:

1 Lettuce. At the harvest festival the priests offered a holy bull some corn. If it ate the corn then that was a good sign – but not for the bull. It was then slaughtered and eaten! The priests also offered a holy lettuce to the God Min. Lettuce was supposed to be a love potion – so offer some to that girl/boy you fancy and see if it works!

2 Pig. Pigs were thought to be unclean. Anyone who accidentally touched one was supposed to run to the nearest river and throw him/herself in – clothes and all! Swineherds were not allowed into temples. That is sow unfair! (Some historians think the Ancient Greek who reported this may have got it a bit wrong, because the Egyptians ate lots of pork.)

3 Barrel of beer. Egyptian women drank as much as the men at parties. You had to drink your host's beer till you were drunk. In fact it was an insult NOT to get drunk. In one tomb painting a woman announces,

I WANT TO DRINK TILL I'M PICKLED. MY GUTS ARE AS DRY AS A STRAW!

Charming lady!

4 Book. The scribes were important people in Egypt and their teachers could be really top people. Egyptian teachers wrote 'The Wisdom of Duauf', a book that contained lots of wise sayings. One of these was:

Three thousand years later teachers are STILL saying that! (Or it could simply be that your teachers are three thousand years old.)

5 Woman. Usually women were not allowed to be priests – a bit like the Christian church until the end of the twentieth century. But around 1000 BC one of the pharaoh's daughters became a priest.

6 Statue. The pharaoh's sister-in-law was ill and her family begged him to send a statue of the Egyptian moon god, Khonsu. He did and it worked. Remember that next time you pig out on too much chocolate cake and become ill: all you need is a statue!

7 Severed hand. Egyptian soldiers chopped off the right hands of dead enemies. This allowed the pharaohs to count the number of dead. Sometimes they cut off the enemies' naughty bits and Egyptian war paintings often show piles of these stacked up! King Menephta of Egypt once took home the naughty bits of 1,300 Libyan soldiers killed in a battle that he won.

8 Bag of corn. And in the reign of Ramesses III the workers didn't get their corn on time. They went on strike – the first strike in history. Corny but true.

9 Wooden beard. Of course the pharaoh was the number-one priest – and priests had no hair. The king showed he was really grown-up by having a beard. How do you have a beard if you have no hair? Wear a false one,

made of wood or woven plant-fibre. It was hung on wires from a band around his forehead. When he died he swapped it for a godly beard – one that is plaited and turned up at the ends. Very fashionable in heaven, of course.

HEY! COOL BEARD PHARAOH DUDE

10 Leopard. Usually priests would wear no animal skin at all – no leather sandals or belts. But the skin of a leopard (or a cheetah) was worn by the chief priest. It was worn like a cloak with the head of the animal hanging over his right shoulder. Grr-reat idea.

Awful army

Egypt suffered a lot from invasions by bandits (who wanted to pinch their cattle). They suffered attacks from tribes like 'the Sea People', who had lost their own land, and from other nations, like the Hittites, who wanted the power and wealth of Egypt.

Being an Egyptian soldier could be hard work. In 1381 BC Amenhotep III's son crushed a revolt in Nubia. In just one hour the Egyptian soldiers captured and massacred 1,000 Nubians.

It was chop till you drop.

But a soldier's life may not have been as bad as Egyptian writers tried to make out. One Egyptian school book said…

The common soldier has many, many officers all telling him what to do. The officers say things like, "Get the men to work!" So the common soldier is woken after just an hour's sleep and worked until sunset. He is always hungry. He is a dead man yet he lives.

Around 1190 BC a teacher wrote...

> A soldier is taken to an army camp while he is still a child. There he is given a beateng. A wound is cut over his eyebrows. His head is split open with a wound. He is laid on the floor and trampled like reed-paper. When he goes to war he is loaded down like an ass till his back is breaking. He drinks foul water and gets to the battle like a plucked chicken.

Fighting fellers

How much do you know about the pharaoh's fighting fellers. Try this tricky test.

Which is the odd one out in these groups?

1 A soldier's weapons were: a stone-headed club, a spear, a bronze axe, a poison dart blower.

2 A common soldier protected himself with: a shield, a mop of thick hair, a helmet, a linen apron.

3 When the army wasn't at war the soldiers had other jobs: policemen, messengers, palace guards, firemen.

4 A soldier's chariot had: tyres, weapon-racks, doors, two horses.

5 An Egyptian army travelled with: laundry women, weapon-makers, cooks, writers.

Answers:

The odd ones out are:

1 A poison dart blower. The main weapon was the club (known today as a 'mace') to beat your enemy's brains out.

2 A helmet. Only the officers had helmets. The ordinary soldiers grew their hair thick to take the club blows and wore an apron to protect their naughty bits. Apart from that they didn't wear much – not even shoes.

3 Firemen. The Egyptians had a good messenger service and soldiers took news from fortress to fortress so the pharaoh always knew what was happening. These forts were about 80 kilometres apart. They also used soldiers as a police force and of course to parade as the pharaoh's guardsmen.

4 Doors. The Egyptians learned from Asia how to use horses, but never rode them in battle – they only used them to pull chariots. Their chariots usually carried a driver and a warrior. The floor was made of woven leather because a solid floor would have given a bouncy, travel-sick-making ride. The wheels had leather tyres to hold them together. (They didn't have strong glue and screws in those days!)

5 Laundry women. As the soldiers only wore an apron they didn't need anyone to do their washing for them. But they did take an army of cooks and weapon-makers and porters to carry their food and beer.

Dodgy Djehuty

Pharaoh Tuthmosis III made the Egyptians masters of the Middle East. But he did it with the help of generals like Djehuty.

Djehuty knew what all good generals know – if you can't win a battle fair and square, then cheat.

The town of Joppa rebelled and Djehuty realized that it would be nearly impossible to capture it by fighting fair. So this is what he did…

1 Djehuty went to Pharaoh Tuthmosis and said he could capture Joppa with just 200 men, 200 wine jars and 200 donkeys.

2 Djehuty went to Joppa and made a camp outside the city. He disguised himself as a messenger and took a letter to the Prince of Joppa. The message said that General Djehuty wanted to betray Egypt and join Joppa. It invited the Prince to meet the general in his camp.

3 Djehuty then went back to camp and dressed himself as the top Egyptian general (which he was). The Prince of Joppa arrived with his bodyguards and the two men chatted alone in a tent. The prince was desperate to know about the magic staff.

4 What happened next was that Djehuty smashed the staff down on the Prince's head and knocked him senseless[13].

5 Djehuty stuffed the stunned Prince into a bag. Then he dressed himself in the Prince's robes and spoke to the bodyguards. He told them that he had captured Djehuty and he wanted them to take the 200 donkeys and the 200 wine jars into Joppa.

13 The prince didn't have much sense to be knocked senseless. Fancy falling for a trick like that.

6 Djehuty told them that the Egyptian army had run away once they knew their general had been captured. Sure enough there wasn't an Egyptian soldier in sight. So the bodyguard set off back to the city. They led the 200 donkeys with the 200 jars up to the gates.

7 As soon as the donkeys were inside the city the Joppa soldiers started to smash the jars. But out of each jar leapt an Egyptian soldier, fully armed.

8 Djehuty threw off his prince disguise and slashed open the bag. He dragged out the real Prince and held a sword to his throat.

9 The soldiers of Joppa fell to their knees and surrendered. Djehuty raised the flag of Egypt over the city.

10 So Joppa was captured and Djehuty became a hero. He'd conquered the city and no one had been hurt.

Oh, all right ... HARDLY anyone was hurt.

Of course the story is very similar to the Wooden Horse of Troy.

Is it true? Is it a legend? You decide…

Quick Egyptian quiz

Do you have a fair old brain (or even a pharaoh brain)? Or are you a mummy's boy? Test yourself with these quaint questions.

1 Pilgrims came to Egypt like holiday-makers to Blackpool. What miniature mummies did they buy as souvenirs? (Clue: did they have to kill these creatures nine times?)

2 Egyptian gods were often pictured with animal heads. Hapy had a baboon's head and Qebehsenuef had a falcon's. But Horemheb was buried with a rare god who had what sort of head? (Clue: flipping tortoise!)

3 The god Khnum created the first Egyptian people. What did he make them from? (Clue: they were earthy people.)

4 Farmers scattered corn on their fields. How did they trample the seed in so the birds couldn't eat it all? (Clue: they were seen and herd.)

5 Another way to keep birds off crops was to use scarecrows. These scarecrows were cleverer than modern ones as they could run around screaming! How?

6 The Egyptians made houses from bricks. The bricks were made from mud mixed with straw or something else. What? (Clue: not to be sniffed at.)

7 A weaver who took a day off work would be punished. How? (Clue: you can't beat it.)

8 Priests shaved off all their hair and eyebrows. Why? (Clue: not such a lousy idea.)

9 After reigning for 30 years a pharaoh would have to prove his strength. How? (Clue: it was a good idea in the long run.)

10 How many sides has an Egyptian pyramid?

Answers:

1 Mummified cats. The cats had their necks broken then were wrapped like a pharaoh's mummy. Pilgrims offered the cats to the gods. Vast cemeteries have been discovered with many thousands of these cat burials. It is likely that the animals were specially bred for this purpose. By 1900 hundreds of TONS of mummified cats had been shipped to Liverpool to be ground up and used as fertiliser.

Horrible Histories note: Some school books tell you the Egyptians mummified their cats because they loved their cute little Tiddles so much! Nice idea – load of rubbish.

2 A turtle. This was not a common statue in Egypt so Horemheb probably had to shell out a lot of money for it!

3 Mud. The early Egyptians called themselves 'black-landers' because they believed they were made from the dark, rich soil by the River Nile. Khnum, they said, breathed life into them and the mud became human beings. Muddy marvellous!

OOOH, LOOK AT HIM!

HIS NILE MUD BULGES IN ALL THE RIGHT WAYS

YEAH! NICE ONE KHNUM

4 With a herd of sheep, goats or pigs. These herds ran around the field and trampled in the grain. Don't try this at home.

5 Because the Egyptians used children as scarecrows. Nowadays we'd probably use traffic wardens because they are scarier than anything.

6 Animal droppings. Poo! Imagine if your house was made of mud mixed with animal droppings! Maybe it is! And imagine mixing it in those days before rubber gloves had been invented. They also burned animal droppings to make a fire.

7 He was beaten. Miss a day's work, weaver, and you get 50 lashes. And weaving was a tough job – you worked all day with your knees drawn up to your chest.

8 To keep free of lice. Everyone from pharaoh to peasant suffered from lice in their hair. Priests became slapheads (and slap-foreheads) to keep clean.

9 He had to run around his palace. Some historians believe that in the early days of Egypt, if the king failed the test he would be sacrificed. He was literally running for his life!

10 Two. An in-side and an out-side. (Oh, come on! This is a *Horrible Histories* book! What did you expect? A FAIR question?)

Cool Cleo

The last great Queen of Egypt was Cleopatra. The Greeks had conquered Egypt 250 years previously and she was the end of the line ... the sticky end.

Cool Cleo facts

1 Cleo was probably not a beautiful woman. She had a long hooked nose, a thick neck and looked more like a man.

2 Cleo was clever. She spoke nine languages and was the first of her family to speak Egyptian.

3 The Egyptians treated her like a pharaoh even though she was from a Greek family and a woman. She worshipped the gods of Egypt.

4 Cleo took the throne when she was about 17 years old in 51 BC. She then married her brother, Ptolemy XIII, who was about 12.

5 The Roman general Pompey was in trouble with Julius Caesar and fled to Egypt. He landed in 48 BC ... and was murdered as he stepped ashore. Little Ptolemy XIII watched.

6 Julius Caesar landed a few days later. Cleo had a long carpet rolled out for him. Cleo was wrapped in the carpet. Surprise! Surprise!

7 Ptolemy XIII ran away when he saw sister Cleo siding with the Romans. He drowned in the Nile as he fled. Cleo simply married brother Ptolemy XIV but her real love was Julius Caesar.

8 When Ptolemy XIV was no more use to her she had him poisoned. Thanks Sis. But Caesar was murdered in Rome.

9 Cleo married new Roman leader Mark Antony in 37 BC but they weren't a popular couple. Mark Antony was attacked by a Roman army and he blamed Cleo for his defeat.

10. To escape his anger she locked herself in her treasure house and sent a message that read 'Cleopatra is dead.'

What happened next is one of the most famous stories in history.

Antony heard Cleo was dead. He went to his room, crying that he would soon be with Cleopatra.

He told his servant Eros…

Antony had himself carried to her treasure house. Cleo was afraid to open the door in case the Romans rushed in, but she and her two serving women let down ropes from a window and pulled him up.

Cleopatra laid Antony on her bed but it was no good … he died.

Cleo locked the doors to her treasure house and refused to come out. When the Roman leader Octavian and his men arrived, Cleopatra refused to let them in. She talked with them through the locked door.

But Octavian was sneaky – he kept her talking while his men set up ladders and climbed through the window.

When Cleo saw the men she pulled out a dagger and tried to stab herself – she missed and was taken prisoner. Her children were taken prisoner too.

Octavian let Cleopatra arrange Antony's funeral. She buried him, then collapsed, sick with a broken heart.

And Cleopatra DID die. But how? Maybe not the way they tell you in the history books. There are TWO tales of her death…

The usual story – Cleo and the awful asp

Here is the history-book story…

a) Cleo wanted to kill herself, but Octavian had her watched.

b) One day he visited her and she flung herself at his feet and told him she wanted to live.

c) Cleo ordered a feast. A man arrived with a basket of figs. Octavian's guards checked the basket and found nothing wrong with it, so they let the man in.

d) After she had eaten, Cleopatra wrote a letter to Octavian. It said…

Then she pressed the asp to her arm.

Octavian sent messengers to stop her killing herself. They came too late. They found her dead on her golden bed, with her maid Iras dying at her feet. Her other maid, Charmion, was putting Cleo's crown on her head. And she soon fell over dead too.

e) Two pricks were found on Cleopatra's arm, and it was believed that she had allowed herself to be bitten by an asp.

She was buried with Mark Antony as she had asked.

We don't know what happened to the asp.

You get the picture. Maybe you've heard the story. It is told in the play by William Shakespeare, *Antony and Cleopatra*.

It's one of the most famous love stories in history ... but is it true?

Maybe all the history books got it wrong![14]

14 This is a *Horrible Histories* book, of course. We swear we will stab ourselves in the stomach with a rusty banana if we get it wrong.

The other story – Cleo and the murder mystery

No one wrote about Cleo's death when it happened. The story of the asp was written 100 years after she died.

Maybe Cleo DIDN'T kill herself. Here's why…

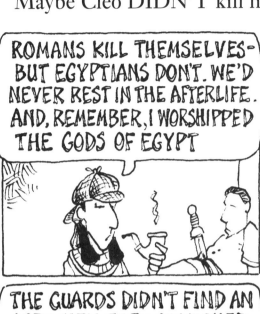

Quick question

Cleopatra and Julius Caesar had a son, Caesarion. Octavian was now emperor and he wanted Caesarion dead. He gave orders that the boy should be strangled. But who did the strangling?

a) The Emperor's cook, who was expert at strangling chickens for dinner.

b) Caesarion's teacher.

c) The Emperor's special assassin, who practised by strangling camels?

Answer: b) Yes, Caesarion was strangled by his own teacher. Would you believe it?

Epilogue

The Ancient Egyptians were amazing people. They lived in the Stone Age, when many humans elsewhere in the world did nothing but grunt and hunt.

They were led by clever and powerful pharaohs – maybe the cleverest people on Earth at that time. They managed to build massive pyramids then set off to conquer as much of the world as they wanted.

There was one thing that drove those phantastic pharaohs on – fear of death if they'd led a wicked life.

A pharaoh would tell you…

They were sure that a person simply left this world and went on to another life.

If you had been a GOOD person then you went on to a better life.

One prayer was written in 1550 BC and it showed just how good you had to be. Would YOU be good enough? The prayer promised the gods…

1. PRAISE AM-KHAIBIT, I HAVE NEVER KILLED A MAN OR A WOMAN
2. PRAISE UTU-NESERT, I HAVE NEVER SWORN
3. PRAISE NEBA, I HAVE NEVER TOLD A LIE
4. PRAISE HER-F-HA-F, I HAVE NEVER MADE ANYONE WEEP
5. PRAISE BASTI, I HAVE NEVER EATEN ANY HEART
6. PRAISE TA-RETIU, I HAVE NEVER ATTACKED ANYONE
7. PRAISE KHEMIU, I HAVE NOT BROKEN THE LAW
8. PRAISE SHET-KHERU, I HAVE NEVER LOST MY TEMPER
9. PRAISE SER-KHERU, I HAVE NEVER STIRRED UP TROUBLE
10. PRAISE AHI, I HAVE NEVER RAISED MY VOICE

How many would you score out of ten? If you can say yes to everything on the list then you can go to the good afterlife.

TEN OUT OF TEN!

ER-THAT'S A NUMBER THREE, I THINK, WAYNE

If you'd been a BAD person you went on to torment and misery. But at least your spirit lived on…

But worst of all was to have your body destroyed. Then your spirit would be homeless and that would be a disaster.

That's why the posh people went to so much trouble to make mummies and make thief-proof tombs.

They failed. Every tomb was robbed – many mummies were wrecked.

For all their brains the pharaohs forgot one important thing – how greedy and ruthless their poor peasants could be.

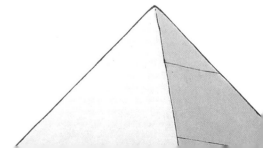

AWESOME EGYPTIAN ACTIVITIES AND GRISLY QUIZZES

Phunny pharaohs

Around 5000 BC the Awesome Egyptians moved into the land by the River Nile. Every year the river flooded and left lovely squidgy mud covering the fields for a few miles on either side – lovely squidgy mud that was good for growing crops. Sound familiar?

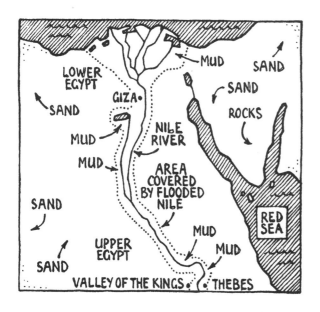

The people of the Nile could usually grow enough food to live – but they were always worried that one year the Nile would let them down and they'd all starve. So they invented gods and prayed that the gods would make the Nile flood.

Then along came some really clever people who said, 'Actually, we are those gods you pray to! So give us lots of food, build us palaces, worship us and we'll look after you!' These really clever people became known as 'pharaohs' – probably because they had a 'fair-old' life with peasants slaving for them![1]

Some historians reckon the Pharaohs came from where?

a) They were chiefs of villages who conquered other villages till they had a kingdom.

b) They were invaders from another country who defeated the Egyptians and ruled them.

c) They were spacemen who landed, defeated the Egyptians and ruled the peasants.

1 Actually, 'Pharaoh' is the Egyptian word for 'Great House'. The peasants didn't dare to speak the name of their king so they called him 'The Great House' – a bit like a Brit calling the queen, 'Mrs Buckingham Palace' or an American calling the president 'Mr White House'.

What is an Awesome Egyptian?

The awesome Egyptians weren't just fabulous pharaohs and mean mummies! Ninety per cent of ancient Egyptians were peasants who worked very hard. Peasants were like property – if a pharaoh gave land to a nobleman then the peasants were thrown in as well.

There were few slaves in Egypt, but if you were a peasant you may as well have been one! Peasants were counted along with the cattle to show how rich a landowner was. Women were not counted because they were not worth as much as cattle!

Below are the peasants and cattle that work on Ali Fayed's land.
Can you find them in the picture above and work out how rich he is?

TOTAL

Pharaoh phoul phacts

The Egyptian people had been around for such a long time they said the ancient Greeks were 'just children'. The Egyptians were a great nation with great kings called pharaohs, but here are a few phoul and phunny phacts about them that you don't usually learn in school…

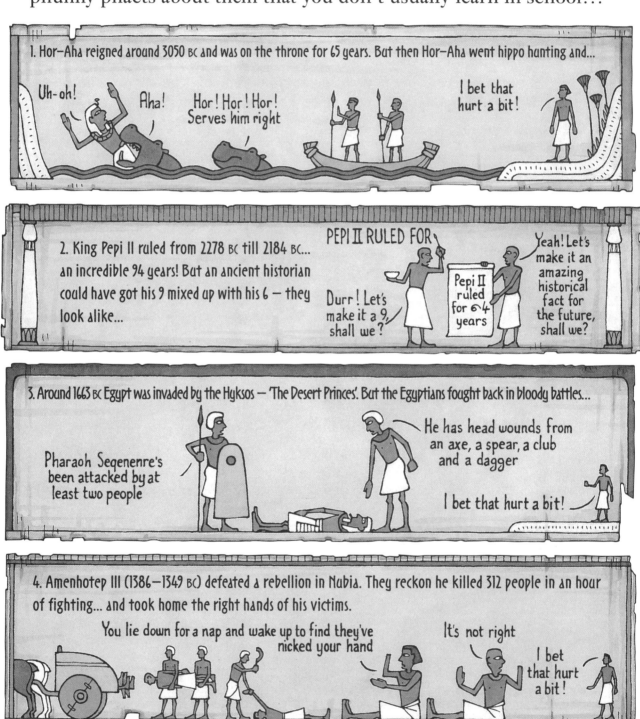

5. Pharaoh Seti (1291–1278 BC) used Hebrew people as slaves. They begged to be set free but he refused... So Hebrew leader Moses called for God to send disasters to Egypt...

Plagues of frogs, cattle diseases, hail storms

OUCH   And boils on the bum

I bet that hurt a bit!

6. Moses led the Hebrews to freedom when God made a path through the 'Red' Sea... But actually it was the REED Sea — a shallow lake. An east wind made a dry path for them to cross. And the wind dropped as the Egyptians chased the Hebrews — it drowned them!

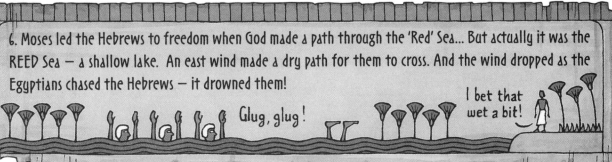

Glug, glug!

I bet that wet a bit!

7. One of the greatest kings of Egypt was Rameses II, who died in 1212 BC. Then the mummy-makers tried a new trick to keep his nose in shape under the bandages...

Stuff his nose full of peppercorns

An idea that's not to be sneezed at!

8. In the 520s BC General Phanes betrayed the Egyptians by switching to the Persian enemy. But Phanes had left his sons behind at the mercy of the Egyptians. The Egyptians showed the lads to Phanes on the battlefield...

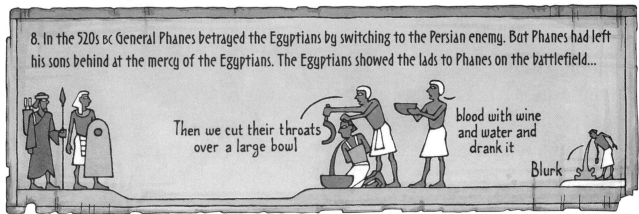

Then we cut their throats over a large bowl

blood with wine and water and drank it

Blurk

135

Mummy-making

The men who made dead bodies into mummies were called embalmers. They took the bodies to a place called the Beautiful House to work on them. Here's how to make a mummy. Unfortunately some words have been mixed up by a mummy's curse. Can you unscramble them?

1) Take the body to a Beautiful House–that's an open-ended NETT in the open air–so the disgusting smells are blown away!

2) Put the body on a wooden table with barsof wood (not a solid top) so you can reach underneath to BEADNAGS it.

3) Remove the brain by pushing a CHILES up the nose to break through, then hook the brain out with a piece of wire.

4) Throw the brain away and pack the skull with 'natron'–a sort of salt that stops bodies GINTROT.

5) Rip open the front of the body and take out the liver, the stomach, the intestines and the lungs – but leave the EARTH inside.

6) Wash the liver, the HOTSCAM, the intestines and the lungs in wine and place them in their sealed canopic jars.

7) Soak the body in natron for 70 days till it is well DECK LIP.

8) Stuff the empty body with rags to give it the right HEAPS, then sew it up.

9) WARP the body in bandages from head to foot.

10) Perform the ceremony of the 'Opening of the HUM TO'–or the mummy won't be able to eat, drink or speak in the next life!

The Egyptians were very superstitious. They also believed in lucky charms. Here is one you could make for yourself out of card to wear around your neck. The three symbols are Egyptian hieroglyphic signs for three words…

'all'   'life' 'protection'

Intestines can be pretty messy, so it's best to tidy them into a special container. The Egyptians made theirs out of clay. You can make one from a drinks bottle.

To make a canopic jar, you will need:
- An empty plastic drinks bottle
- Paints or felt-tip pens or pencils
- Modelling clay
- Drawing paper
- Sticky tape or glue
- Sand or pebbles

1) Take the top off the drinks bottle and rinse it out.
2) Put some sand or pebbles in the bottle to stop it falling over.
3) Decorate the paper with hieroglyphs and Egyptian pictures and symbols.

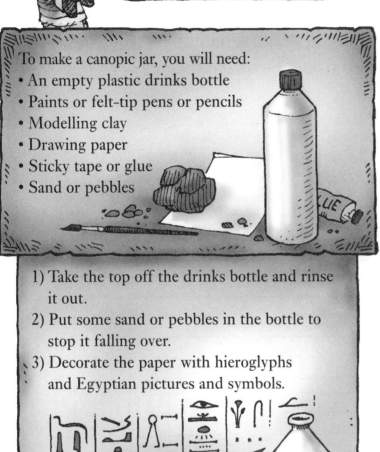

4) Wrap the paper round the bottle.
5) Tape or glue the paper to the bottle.

I THINK WE'LL NEED A BIGGER CANOPIC JAR

6) Use the modelling clay to make a lid. Make the lid into the shape of one of the four Sons of Horus (see below).
7) Make all four jars to complete the set.

DUAMUTEF

QEBEHSENUEF

IMSETY

HAPI

Fate of the mummy

After the pharaoh was turned into a mummy, they would be placed in a coffin in a tomb which was sealed. This was to shut out the grave-robbers. The dead person would then have to pass through a dangerous place known as the Duat. The dangers were monsters, boiling lakes and rivers of fire. The snake that spat poison was particularly nasty.

The monsters that live in the Duat could be overcome with the right spells. The spells were written down on Egyptian paper (papyrus) and left near the coffin. This is the 'Book of the Dead.' Can you help the dead pharaoh find his way through the Duat to the gates of Yaru (the Egyptian afterlife)?

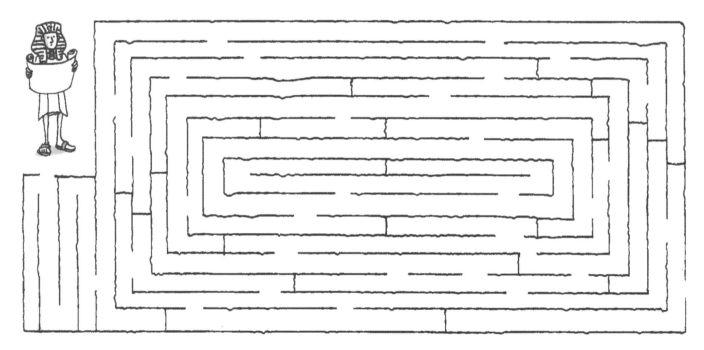

At the gates of Yaru, the pharaoh's heart was placed in one side of a balance and in the other side was the Feather of Truth (this held all the lies of your past life). If the heart was lighter than the feather, the dead person was allowed through the gates. But if it was heavier … their heart was eaten by the Devourer. Colour in the dotted areas to find out what this terrifying monster looked like.

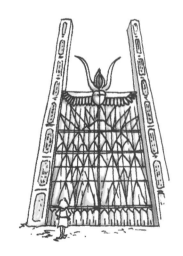

The Egyptians mummified more than their pharaohs. They mummified the pharaohs' pets and buried them in the pyramids to keep the dead kings company in the afterlife. Look at these two pictures. Spot ten differences between the two and circle them with a pencil.

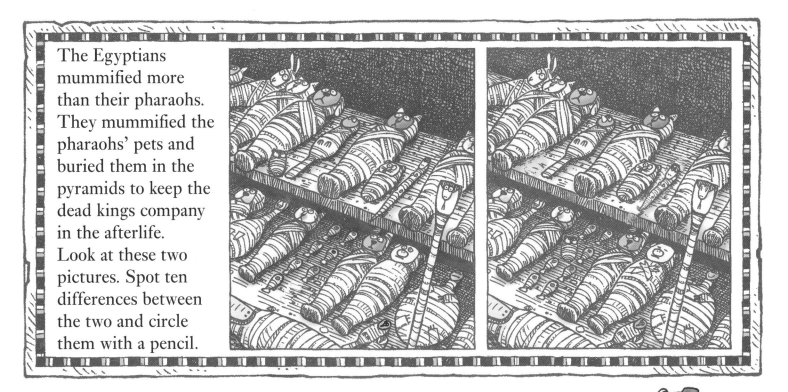

Pilgrims came to ancient Egypt like holiday-makers to Blackpool. They bought miniature mummies as souvenirs. To find out exactly what the Egyptians bought, answer all 5 questions below. Use your answers to work your way around the puzzle. You should only make words from letters that are next to each other. The letters that remain will give you the answer.

1) A magician pulls this long-eared creature out of a hat: _ _ _ _ _ _ (6)

2) When you're looking for a compliment you are said to be _ _ _ _ing for one. (4)

3) Man's best friend: _ _ _ (3)

4) If your bedroom's in a mess, your mum would call it a _ _ _sty! (3)

5) When you go under a very low bridge you should _ _ _ _ to avoid hitting your head. (4)

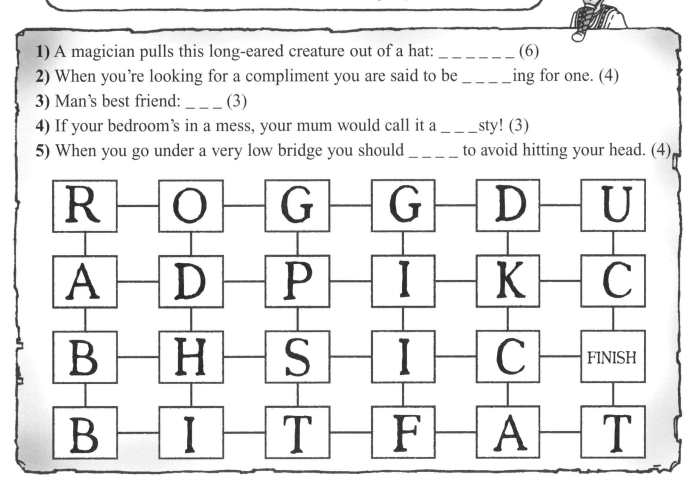

139

Gruesome grave-robbers

Pyramids were filled with goodies so the pharaohs would be as rich in the next life as they were in this life. Of course they've all been robbed now – some were robbed at the time of the burial and the rest have been cleaned out by greedy treasure hunters in the twentieth century.

> *Pharaohs eventually realized that a pyramid was a huge stone advert saying, "Look at my grave! Look at my wealth!" The only answer was to hide the tombs. The pharaohs switched to being buried in hidden caves in the rocks. Help this grave-robber find the correct path that leads to the pharaoh's treasure.*

Cast yourself back in time a few thousand years. You are travelling through ancient Egypt and you've run out of copper coins. You want to rob a pyramid or a rock tomb (and get away with it). Answer Yes or No to the questions below and turn to page 155 to see if you have what it takes to become a successful grave-robber.

1) Do you do all the work yourself so that you get to keep all the loot?

2) Will you have to spend money to get people on your side?

3) Is it a good idea to go through the front entrance of the pyramid?

4) Should you bribe everyone concerned with the burial?

5) Is setting fire to the tomb a good idea?

6) As a grave-robber, should you avoid travelling merchants?

7) Should you spend your treasure so there's no evidence that it was you?

8) Is it easy to find your way around the inside of a pyramid?

9) Should you try to steal the body before it is buried?

10) Will you be punished if you get caught?

Many tomb-builders became grave-robbers. They grew hungry when their wages were late. They tried going on strike and marching on the officials' houses with chants of, "We are hungry! We are hungry!" When that failed they turned to robbing the tombs they'd helped to build. Look at the two scenes below. Spot eight differences between the two and circle them with a pencil.

Curious curses

Mummies are a bit creepy. Looking at corpses of long-dead people is enough to give you goose-bumps on your goose-bumps! But it's not creepy enough for some people. They imagine the mummies aren't just shrivelled flesh – they believe the mummy spirits wander around. These spirits bring curses and spells to the living people who disturb their rest and rob their graves.

Lots of 'true' mummy stories have been told over the past century. This is one of them – see if you believe it! Count Louis Hamon wrote to his friend, Lord Carnarvon. He begged him to be careful on his expedition in Egypt. Put the pictures in the right order to find out why Louis Hamon wanted to warn his friend.

Fill in the grid below with the correct sequence.

Lord Carnarvon ignored his friend's letter. His expedition found the fabulous tomb of Tutankhamun and seven weeks after that, Lord Carnarvon was dead! He got a mosquito bite on his left cheek which became infected. When doctors examined Tutankhamun's mummy, they noticed a strange mark– on his left cheek! Copy the picture boxes into the grid to see the full picture.

1	2	3	4
5	6	7	8
9	10	11	12
13	14	15	16

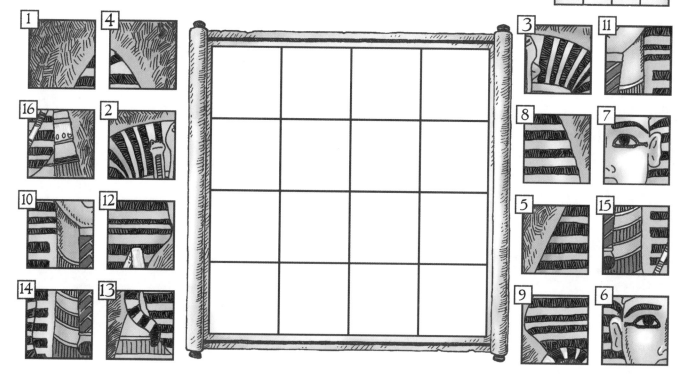

The death of Lord Carnarvon was one of the first stories about the Curse of Tutankhamun's Tomb. Each of the following six stories has been told by someone at some time. Can you work out which stories are simply LIES, which are MISTAKES and which are TRUE but can be explained?

1) Arthur Mace was one of the first to enter the tomb and he died shortly after.

2) When Tutankhamun's mummy was unwrapped, the archaeologists found a curse wrapped in the bandages. It said: 'They who enter this sacred tomb shall swiftly be visited by the wings of death.'

3) When Lord Carnarvon died, his favourite dog howled and died at the exact moment of his death. The dog was 3,000 miles away in England.

4) A worker in the British Museum was fastening labels to things stolen from Tutankhamun's tomb. He dropped dead shortly after.

5) American millionaire George Gould visited the tomb. He was fine before he went, but died the next day.

6) The mummy's 'curse' is in fact ancient Egyptian germs that were sealed into the tomb 3,000 years ago.

Gruesome gods

Egyptians wanted to reach the spirit world that the priests taught about. There was an awesome number of gods for an Egyptian to please before he or she got there. And if they annoyed one, well, it was tombs-full of trouble for them!

Egyptian gods were unbelievably old. They had lived before people existed and now treated humans as if they were a mixture of toys and servants. The gods controlled the world and everything that happened. They demanded respect. Can you match the images of the gods below to their descriptions?

A

L

1) Anubis – the jackal-headed god of the dead. He helped to prepare mummies.

2) Bes – the dwarf god of happiness, and protector of the family.

3) Hathor – the cow-horned goddess of love. She also looked after happiness, dancing and music.

4) Horus – the falcon-headed god who looked after the pharaoh.

5) Isis – wife of Osiris. She took special care of women and children.

K

6) Osiris – god of death and rebirth, the Underworld and the Earth. Long ago he had taught people to farm.

7) Ptah – the god who spoke the names of all the things in the world. By doing this he made them exist.

8) Re – the Sun God. Some said he had made people. The Egyptians called themselves, 'the cattle of Re'.

9) Seth – god of the desert and storms. The enemy of Osiris.

J

10) Sekhmet – the lioness goddess of war.

11) Sobek – the crocodile-headed god. He controlled water supplies.

12) Thoth – the ibis-headed god of wisdom who invented speaking and writing.

B

C

D

E

F

G

H

I

Need an awesome answer to a powerful problem? Read the Dear God… letters below and use the list of gods on page 6 to work out which god each person is praying to.

1) Oh great _____. My land is short of water and my crops are dying.

2) Mighty _____. My youngest son died of fever three months ago. Since then my wife is heart-broken. Please help her to enjoy life again.

3) Oh wise _____. My son wishes to be a scribe, but he is so bad at learning his hieroglyphs that his teachers are threatening to throw him out of school. Beatings don't seem to help.

4) Please give me strength, oh vengeful _____. Raiders from the Red Land have attacked our village. Help us to defeat them.

5) Please, sweet _____. I am madly in love with the most beautiful girl, but she laughs at my dancing. I am terribly clumsy and fall over my own feet.

> ERRR!

> GO ON! DO YOU WANT TO DANCE WITH HER OR DON'T YOU!?

Most awesome Egyptian myths have various versions of the same story. Here is one version of the Isis and Osiris story. Sadly our suffering scribe has scrambled the terrible tale in places. Can you unscramble the words in CAPITAL LETTERS?

Osiris was an awesome king. He was loved by his loyal wife, Isis, and all of his people. Only Osiris's brother, Set, hated him. He was LASOUJE of his brother and planned to kill him.

Set DOINGEARS a large feast. At the height of the festivities, Set produced a casket and ACNDOENUN that it would be given to whoever it fitted. All the guests tried the casket for size, but none fitted, until finally, Osiris stepped into the casket. Set slammed the lid closed and sealed the casket shut with boiling lead. The SALDEE coffin was then thrown into the Nile.

Isis SEHCRAED for the casket all over Egypt. At last, she found it where it had come to rest in the roots of a huge tree.

Isis took the coffin back for a proper ALIRUB. For safety, she hid it in the marshes beside the Nile. Sneaky Set found the casket and was so GEDENRA he chopped the body of Osiris into pieces, and RECAEDSTT the parts throughout the land of Egypt.

Poor Isis set out again looking for the bits of her husband. At last, she found all the parts except one (his naughty bit) and reassembled Osiris and PAREDPW him in bandages. The first mummy!

Osiris was also a daddy and his son, Horus, went out to battle his savage uncle Set. After a series of battles, neither was able to win. In the end, Osiris was made king of the underworld, Horus – king of the living and Set – ruler of the deserts as the god of evil. So they all died happily ever after!

Potty pyramids

Pyramids are H-U-G-E. They were built as graves for the pharaohs after they left this life. They were filled with goodies so the kings would be as rich in the next life as they were in this life.

Not everyone agrees the pyramids are graves, of course. Thinking about those great lumps of dense stone, are people with great lumps of dense brain who have other ideas. But which of the following wacky ideas have some people seriously believed? Answer true or false…

Someone has said that the pyramids are …

1 Adverts. The priests wanted to leave something to show the world how great they were.

2 Simple landmarks. All maps would be drawn with the pyramids at the centre and distances worked out from there.

3 Chambers of horrors. Dead kings were stuck inside, then the Egyptian people were charged two onions an hour to walk around and view their kingly corpses.

4 Sundials. The shadow from the Great Pyramid would be used to work out the time.

5 Fortune-telling machines. They've been used to predict the birth of Christ, the date of World War I and the end of the world – AD 2979 if you're worried.

6 Star calculators. They help to measure the speed of light, the distances from the earth to the sun and to keep a record of the movement of the stars.

7 Calendars. They can measure the length of a year to three decimal places.

8 Star maps. The pyramids are laid out in the same pattern as a cluster of stars called Orion. Of course you could only see this pattern if you are ten miles up in the air – or a Martian in a flying saucer.

9 Centres of invisible forces of the universe. Weird things can happen there – like blunt razors turning sharp and people feeling wobbly at the knees when they enter.

10 Maths calculators. Take the distances around the edges and the angles and whatnot and you can work out the distance round a circle (its circumference) if you know the distance across (its diameter).

> *There are some awesome things you ought to know about the pyramids.*
> *Here is a crossword with a difference – it doesn't have any clues.*
> *The words missing from the facts below make up the answers.*
> *The information in brackets tells you where they should go in the grid.*

1) A pyramid was supposedly built as a huge stone _____ (6 across, 4 letters) of a pharaoh.

2) The burial chamber in the centre was filled with awesome _____ (5 down, 6 letters) for the pharaoh to take into the afterlife.

3) The riches were a temptation to _____ (4 across, 7 letters). The pyramid builders tried to fool the thieves by making false doors, staircases and corridors.

4) The base of the Great Pyramid of Cheops is equal to the area of seven or eight _____ (3 down, 8 letters) pitches (230 metres x 230 metres).

5) The pyramids are close to the _____ (1 down, 4 letters) because some of the huge stones had to be carried from the quarries by boat.

6) The pyramids are all on the west bank of the Nile – the side on which the ___ (7 across, 3 letters) sets. This is for religious reasons.

7) The pyramids were built from enormous stone blocks. But how did the Egyptians _____ (2 across, 4 letters) them when they had no cranes?

147

Powerful pyramids

The Great Pyramid in Giza is made up of about 2,300,000 stone blocks. If you broke the Great Pyramid into slabs 30cm thick, you could build a wall 1 metre high that would stretch all the way around France. If you had a little more time, you could cut the stone into rods about 6cm square – join them together and you'd have enough to reach the Moon!

Can you find the words listed in the pyramids? The words can be found written up, down, backwards and across. Then unscramble the letters in the mini pyramid to work out which civilization lived 5,000 years ago!

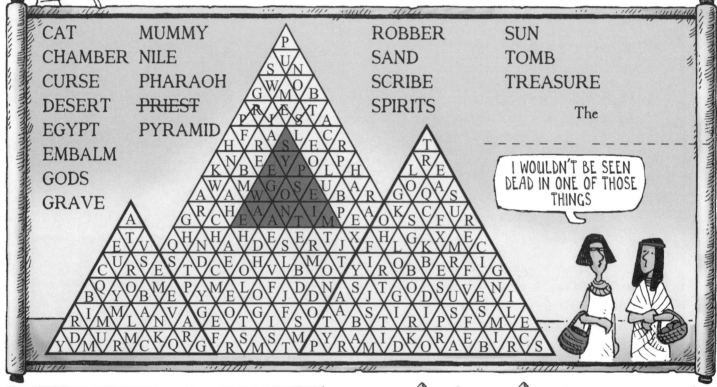

CAT
CHAMBER
CURSE
DESERT
EGYPT
EMBALM
GODS
GRAVE

MUMMY
NILE
PHARAOH
~~PRIEST~~
PYRAMID

ROBBER
SAND
SCRIBE
SPIRITS

SUN
TOMB
TREASURE

The _ _ _ _ _ _ _ _

I WOULDN'T BE SEEN DEAD IN ONE OF THOSE THINGS

DAILY BLAH
(7 January 1993)

STOP PRESS: News Flash

Archaeologists in Egypt have found the ruins of a small pyramid, a few metres from the Great Pyramid of Cheops at Giza. It was discovered by chance during a cleaning operation. This brings the number of known pyramids to 96. Can you count how many overlapping pyramids there are here?

Do you think you could be an artist? Here's your chance to prove yourself. A pharaoh has a new pyramid that needs to be decorated with the picture below. Copy the lines in each square onto the empty grid. Then colour your picture in.

Remember the Egyptian style. Heads are painted sideways, but the eye is shown full face. Legs are shown sideways and both shoulders should be in view. The more important the person, the bigger they are. Pharaoh gets most space.

If you work with some friends you could copy the drawing and make a wall painting. DANGER – don't use the living room wall without first asking … or you could be history.

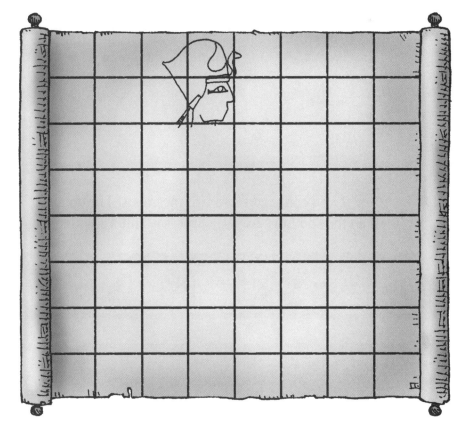

149

Wrotten writing

To be a top man in Egypt you had to be able to read and write. Boys (not girls) had to go to school in the temple and suffer under terrible teachers who worked them and beat them without mercy. In Egypt you had to suffer to succeed.

> *Egyptian writing is called hieroglyphics. Sometimes a hieroglyphic sign means a letter – the way it does in our alphabet. Sometimes it means a whole word. Hieroglyphs were deliberately complicated so that it took a long time to read and write them. It meant that those who could read and write were more important.*

A. vulture

B. leg

D. hand

F. viper

G. pot or stand

CH. rope

I. reed

J. serpent

K. basket

L. lion

M. owl

N. water

P. stool

Q. hill

R. mouth

S. cloth

T. loaf

W. chick

Y. reeds

Z. bolt

Here are some Egyptian hieroglyphs. Use them to write your name. The Egyptians didn't have signs for letters C, E, O, U, V and X, so you will need to add these letters with the hieroglyphs.

FISH, HAND, SQUIGGLE SPELLS CAT

See if you can read these two messages. The sound of the letters is more important than the spelling. Anyway, who says the Egyptians had to be good at spelling? Are you?

EH?

If you think school is bad in the 21st century, you should have gone to school in ancient Egypt. Learning to be a scribe was hard. The teachers were stern and the discipline was strict. Unscramble the words in CAPITAL LETTERS to read this text called 'Advice to a Young Scribe'...

O scribe do not be LIED, or you shall be CRUDES.

Do TON give your EARTH to RULES PEA or you HALLS fail. Do not PENDS a day in SEEN LIDS or you shall be AT BEEN. A YOB'S ear is on his DICE BASK and he listens HEWN he is BEE TAN!

Can you find the list of these hieroglyphs hidden in the grid below? They can be found written up, down, backwards and across. Then try and work out what the hieroglyphs say. If you can, you are on the way to becoming an awesome Egyptian expert!

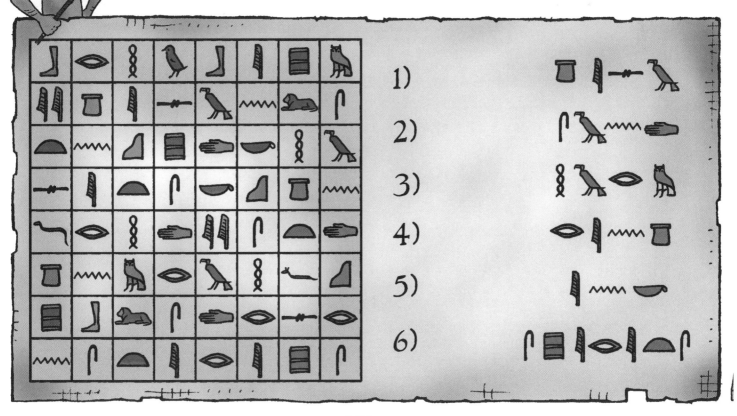

Gory stories

Just because the stories from Ancient Egypt were written down it doesn't mean they were true! Take the story of King Khufu as told by the Egyptians… Find a couple of friends, pick which part you want to play and have a go at being an awesome Egyptian.

  Cast: King Khufu  Djedi the magician Neria the maid

GOOSE MAGIC

Scene 1: In the palace

Khufu: Neria, slave!

Neria: Yes, boss?

Khufu: How is my pyramid coming along? It's going to be the greatest pyramid ever built!

Neria: Oh, it's not coming along at all, boss. The workers won't work because you've run out of money to pay them.

Khufu: What am I to do? It's only half finished. There's no point in having a pyramid without a point. I'll be dead soon.

Neria: Tell you what, boss, I've heard about a bloke called Djedi. Says he's a magician who can bring people back to life. He could keep you going long enough to get the pyramid finished.

Khufu: Good thinking. I'm glad I thought of it. Send for Djedi!

Neria: If you ask me he's a bit of a fake. If you ask me he just does tricks.

Khufu: Well, I'm not asking you. Send for him!

Music and stuff as time passes

Scene 2: In the palace – later

Neria: (To Djedi) You're for it, sunshine. The boss wants you to prove you can bring something back to life – or you'll be bringing yourself back to life.

Djedi: I have a goose here in this box. Killed it this morning. (Lifts headless goose out of box.)

Neria: Very tasty. After you've brought it back to life you can kill it again and I'll have it for me supper.

Khufu: Are you the magician?

Djedi: I am Djedi – the greatest magician the world has ever seen.

Khufu: You'll be the richest magician the world has ever seen if you can bring the dead back to life.

Djedi: I have here a goose…

Khufu: Never mind the goose. Neria – I want you to go to the prison and fetch me a prisoner. We'll kill him and let Djedi here bring him back to life!

Djedi: (Panic) You can't do that! No! You can't! It's against the law. Just let me show you what I can do with this goose!

Khufu: Oh, go on then. A bit boring, but go on.

Djedi: (Puts goose in box and closes lid. Waves hands over box then pulls out live goose.) There you are, Your Highness!

Khufu: Great stuff. Come back when I'm dead and do the same for me. I will reward you with riches beyond your dreams. (Khufu leaves.)

Neria: He nearly caught you there, sunshine!

Djedi: What do you mean?

Neria: I mean the live goose was in the box all the time. You just switched it when you put the dead one back in the box. I'm not stupid like the king, you know. He'll have you executed if he ever finds out.

Djedi: You won't tell him!

Neria: I might … unless…

Djedi: What? What do you want? What is the price of your silence?

Neria: That dead goose for me supper.

Djedi: It's a deal.

Suffering soldiers

An Egyptian soldier's life was probably not as bad as student scribes tried to make out. The young writers wrote charming true-life notes like this one about soldiers:

> The common soldier has many, many officers all telling him what to do. The officers say things like, 'Get the men to work!' So the common soldier is woken after just an hour's sleep and worked until sunset. He is always hungry. He is like a dead man and yet he lives.

A bit like going to school today, isn't it?

Egypt had problems with invasions from bandits (who wanted to pinch their cattle), from tribes like 'The Sea People' who had lost their own land, and from other nations like the Hittites who wanted the power and wealth of Egypt.

The pharaohs needed armies to defend their land. But what do you know about them? Pick out the one *wrong* answer in each list below.

1 A soldier's weapons were...
a stone-headed club, a spear, a bronze axe, a poison dart blower.

2 A common soldier protected himself with...
a shield, a mop of thick hair, a helmet, a linen apron.

3 When soldiers weren't at war they had to work as....
policemen, messengers, palace guards, firemen.

4 A soldier's chariot has...
tyres, weapon-racks, doors, two horses.

5 An Egyptian army travelled with...
laundry women, weapon-makers, cooks, writers.

Grisly quiz

So you think you now know a thing or two about the awesome ancients? Test your knowledge with this multiple choice quiz and see if you're a Horrible Histories expert or not.

1. What percentage of Egyptians lived as slaves, er, sorry, peasants? (Of course, they might as well have been slaves!)
   a) 20%   b) 40%   c) 90%

2. The pharaoh proved his fitness to be king by doing one of the following trials:
   a) killing at least 100 enemies by his own hand within the first five years of his reign
   b) running round a gruelling obstacle course after he'd reigned for 30 years

   c) having at least four children by the end of the tenth year of his reign

3. Gods played a very important role in Egyptian life. Which of these three is actually an Egyptian god?
   a) Re – the Sun God. Some said he made people. The Egyptians called themselves, 'the cattle of Re'.
   b) Ta – the Moon God. Egyptians would howl to Ta when the moon was full.
   c) Bla – the god of the universe. Egyptians made animal sacrifices to him twice a month.

4. Egyptians spent most of their lives worrying about:
   a) taxes
   b) the plague
   c) the afterlife

5. The Egyptians who could read and write were called:
   a) wordsmiths   b) scribes   c) editors

6. Why did Egyptians make their dead (at least the ones who could afford it) into mummies?
   a) to scare away grave robbers
   b) bodies that rotted wouldn't make it into the afterlife
   c) to keep the rats from nibbling on their toes

7. How many pyramids were built in ancient Egypt?
   a) 35   b) 96   c) 57

8. What happened to certain body parts that were taken out of a dead body?
   a) They were put into canopic jars.
   b) They were thrown into the River Nile.
   c) They were burned at the entrance to the pyramid.

9. What do many people believe happened when you robbed a pharaoh's tomb?
   a) The ceiling would collapse on top of you.
   b) You would be cursed by the mummy and probably die.
   c) Your brain would turn to jelly.

Answers

Phunny Pharaohs

Historians have argued that all of these are true! Yes, some fruitcake even said that pharaohs came from outer space. But sensible you will realize a) or b) is more likely.

What is an Awesome Egyptian?

Thirty peasants and cattle work on Ali Fayed's land. Remember, women were not counted.

Mummy-making

TENT, BANDAGES, CHISEL, ROTTING, HEART, STOMACH, PICKLED, SHAPE, WRAP, MOUTH

Fate of the Mummy

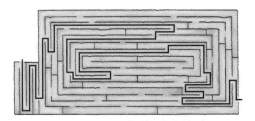

1 = RABBIT   2 = FISH   3 = DOG   4 = PIG   5 = DUCK

Pilgrims bought mummified CATS as souvenirs.

Gruesome grave-robbers

Cast yourself back in time…

1   No. You will need a group of at least 7 or 8 people to help you.

2   Yes. They will help you to enter the tomb and open the coffin.

3   No. You should find a back entrance. With the front entrance untouched, no one will suspect anything's wrong.

4   Yes. You will need the officials and priests to turn a blind eye.

5   Yes. The gold will be melted down, ready for you to move it easily.

6   No. Merchants can buy your stolen treasures–no questions asked.

7   No. Many a grave-robber was caught this way. People wanted to know where all that wealth came from.

8   No. You need to know the passages and rooms as well as a tomb builder.

9   Yes. It could save you a lot of trouble.

10   Yes. You will be tortured and then executed.

Curious curses

Story in the correct sequence: G, A, M, H, B, I, C, F, L, N, D, J, K, O, E

The death of Lord Carnarvon was…

1 = True, but… Mace had been ill before he entered the tomb. He had pleurisy. There were no cures for this illness in 1922.

2 = Lies. A newspaper reported this curse soon after Carnarvon's death.

3 = True, but it's a creepy story told by Lord Carnarvon's son.

4 = Lies. The British Museum never had any objects from Tut's tomb.

5 = Mistake. Gould was not in good health before his visit. He went to Egypt because he was ill, but the stress of travelling killed him.

6 = Mistake. The air in the tomb wouldn't be very healthy, but King Tut's germs wouldn't kill a visitor.

Gruesome gods

Egyptian gods were unbelievably…

1 = J   2 = G   3 = K   4 = A   5 = C   6 = H
7 = E   8 = B   9 = L   10 = I   11 = F
12 = D

Need an awesome answer to a powerful problem?

1 = Sobek   2 = Isis   3 = Thoth
4 = Sekhmet   5 = Hathor

Most awesome Egyptian myths…

Unscrambled words in the correct order: JEALOUS, ORGANISED, ANNOUNCED, SEALED, SEARCHED, BURIAL, ANGERED, SCATTERED, WRAPPED.

Potty pyramids

All except 3 have been believed by someone … usually someone with more thumbnail than brain, but you can believe them if you like. Most people just admit they are huge tombs for dead kings.

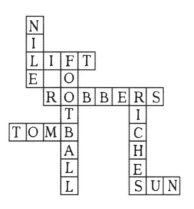

Powerful pyramids

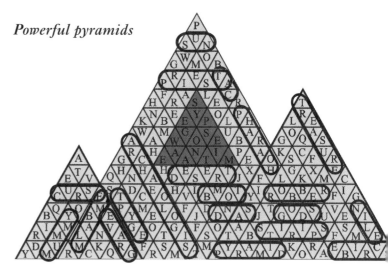

There are 35 overlapping pyramids.

Wrotten writing

See if you can read these two…

Pyramids ar(e) big   My nits ar(e) itchy

If you think school is bad…

Unscrambled words in the correct order: IDLE, CURSED, NOT, HEART, PLEASURE, SHALL, SPEND, IDLENESS, BEATEN, BOY'S, BACKSIDE, WHEN, BEATEN!

Can you find the list…

1) GIZA
2) SAND
3) CHARM
4) RING
5) INK
6) SPIRITS

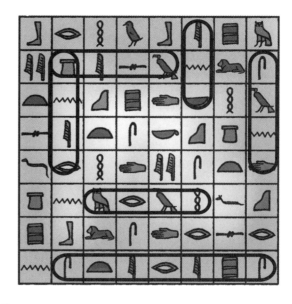

156

Suffering soldiers

1 A poison dart blower. The main weapon was the club (known today as a 'mace') to beat out your enemy's brains.

2 A helmet. Only the officers had helmets. The ordinary soldiers grew their hair thick to take the club blows and wore an apron to protect their naughty bits. Apart from that they didn't even wear shoes.

3 Firemen. The Egyptians had a good messenger service and soldiers took news from fortress to fortress so the pharaoh always knew what was happening. These forts were about 80 kilometres apart. They also used soldiers as a police force and of course to parade as the pharaoh's guards.

4 Doors. The Egyptians learned from Asia how to use horses but never rode them in battle – they only used them to pull chariots. Their chariots usually carried a driver and a warrior. The floor was made of woven leather because a solid floor would have given a bouncy, travel-sick-making ride. The wheels had leather tyres to hold them together. (They didn't have strong glue and screws in those days!)

5 Laundry women. As the soldiers only wore a loincloth, they didn't need anyone to do their washing for them. But they did take an army of cooks and weapon-makers and porters to carry their food and beer.

Grisly quiz

1. c), 2. b), 3. a), 4. c), 5. b), 6. b), 7. b), 8. a), 9. b)

157

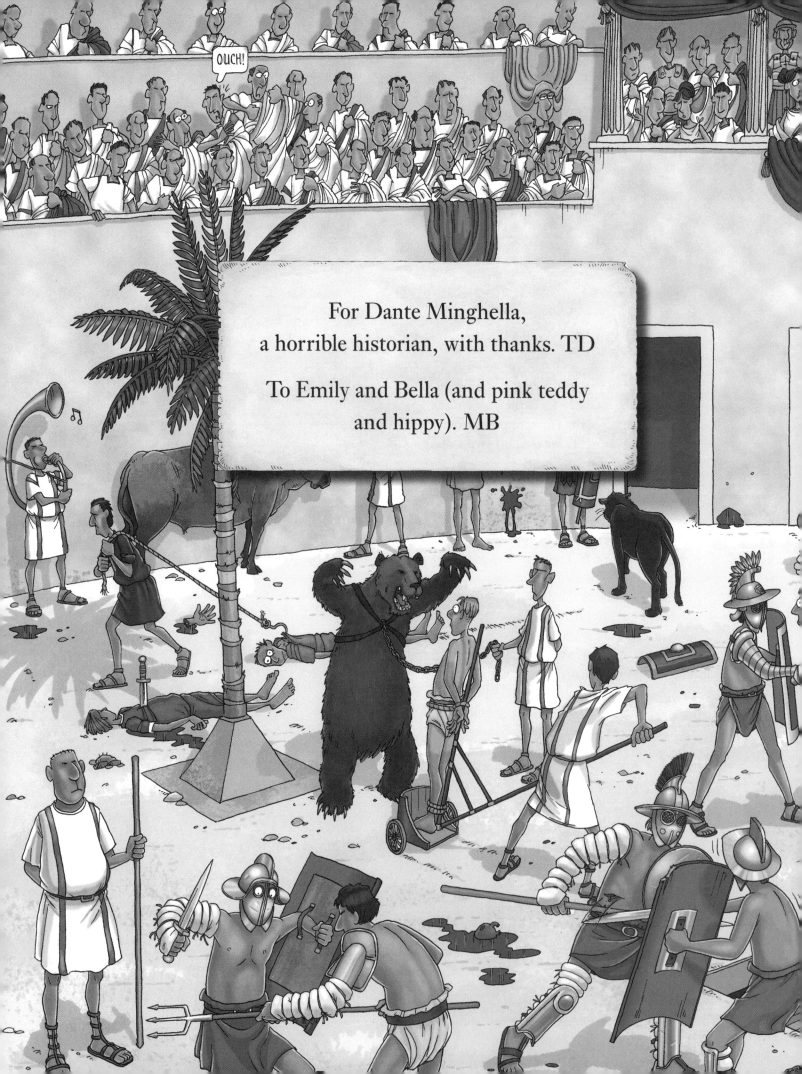

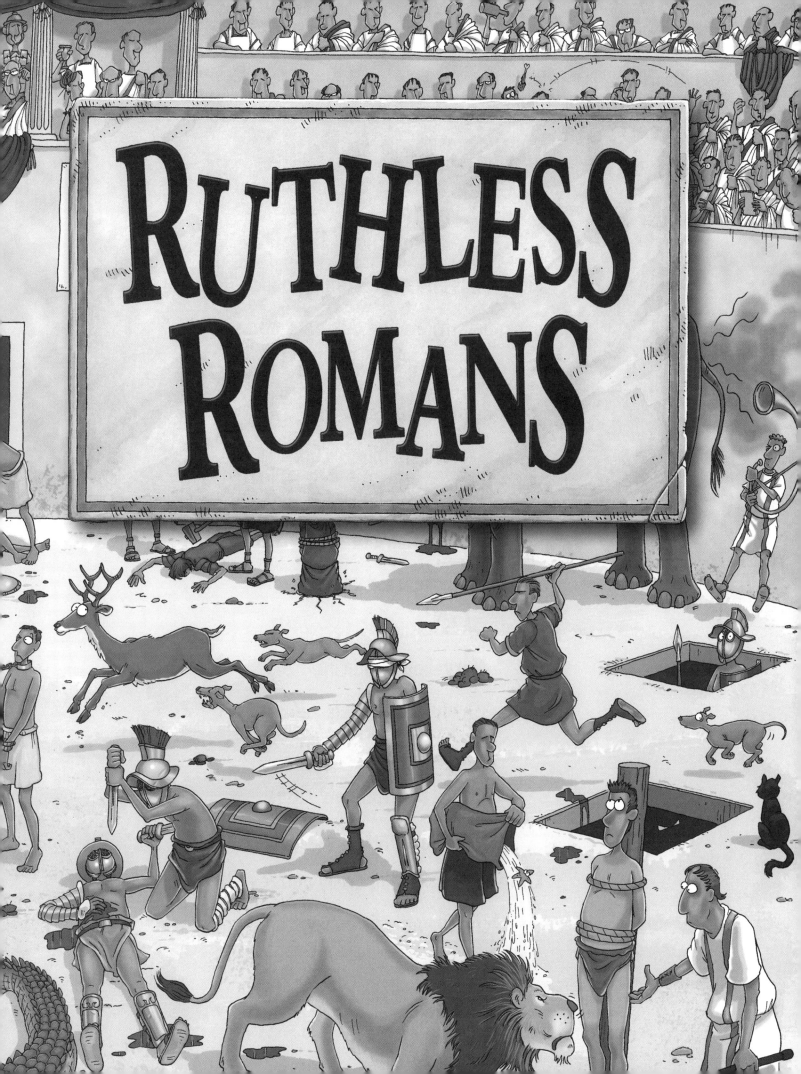

CONTENTS

Introduction

History has always been horrible. But some bits are more horrible than others. So, if there was a contest, who would be the most horrible people in history?

Of course, the Aztecs ripped out hearts because they thought that was the only way to make sure the sun would rise in the morning. They thought they had a good reason!

The Spanish torturers would have told you they were killing their victims – to make sure those victims could go to heaven. They thought they were helping!

Isn't it strange? Teachers and history books try to tell you how great the Roman Empire was...

Teachers often use the word 'civilized' to describe the Romans – that's the opposite to 'wild'.

Yet the Romans did something the heart-ripping Aztecs and the Spanish burners didn't do ... they killed people for *fun*! The Romans made murder into a *sport*. They built wonderful buildings like the Colosseum, filled them with happy Romans and then massacred thousands of people and animals for *entertainment*.

They did lots of other ruthless and disgusting things too. Most history books (and teachers) try to forget the dark and deadly side of the ruthless Romans. What you need is a book that will tell you the *truth*. What you need is a *horrible* history of the ruthless Romans.

Now, I wonder where you'll find a book like that...

Killer kings and the rotten republic

Rome's history is in three parts really...

- First there were Roman 'kings' – war leaders who went around smashing other people. Then the seventh king started smashing his own Roman people so...
- Kings were thrown out and the people ruled themselves – that's called a 'republic'. But the Romans decided one strong leader was better for smashing other people so...
- They created 'emperors' with an 'empire' which smashed everyone in sight ... and many who were out of sight too. It all started back in the distant mists of time in Italy...

Killer kings timeline

1000 BC Rome begins as a collection of villages on seven hilltops near the River Tiber. They are on the hilltops because it is easier to defend them against enemies all around.

753 BC Romulus – a reject from the nearby state of Alba Longa – murders his twin brother, Remus, then marks out a boundary. 'This is a new town and I name it after ... er, me!'

700 BC The seven villages all join together and build a meeting place – a 'forum' in one of the valleys between them – and the seven villages become one city.

673–642 BC Reign of Tullius Hostilius, third king of Rome. He sets about attacking neighbours Alba Longa.

642–617 BC The fourth king, Ancus Marcius, makes the city bigger still, and builds the first bridge across the River Tiber. (That will come in *very* handy later for throwing people into the river.) He also builds Ostia at the mouth of that river to turn Rome into a seaport so the Romans can now massacre people on land *and* on the water.

616 BC Tarquinius Priscinus, becomes the fifth king of Rome. The Romans start to spread out and take over their local enemy city Alba Longa. Building starts on great temples and even greater sewers. (You can't make a big city without sewers.)

578–535 BC The sixth king, Servius Tullius, enlarges the city by building a wall around it, five miles long with 19 gates. (Lots of ways out when it comes to getting rid of the corpses of dead Romans later.) And Servius has the first Roman coins stamped with his head on them.

535–510 BC Reign of King Tarquin the Proud (posh name Tarquinius Superbus). Romans have now conquered about 350 square miles.

510 BC Wicked King Tarquin is thrown out of Rome and the city picks its own leaders – it becomes a 'republic'. But some people think

there was no such person as Tarquin the Proud! He was just a made-up man – a fairy tale to warn us about how evil kings can be.

Rotten Romulus and Remus

The legends say the terrible twins, Romulus and Remus, founded Rome in a wonderful (but wacky) way.

The boys were just babies in the state of Alba Longa when their wicked uncle decided to have them killed. They were put in a trough and thrown into the River Tiber. Luckily the trough floated till it was caught on a thorny bush and they landed safely. The lads were cared for by a wolf and a woodpecker.

Then they were rescued and raised by a shepherd. When the brothers grew up they returned to the thorn bush to set up a city. Romulus ploughed a line around the city boundary. 'And don't you dare cross it, Remus,' he told his brother. So what did Remus do? Crossed it. What did Romulus do? Killed him. Problem solved.

Romulus was a bit short of women for his new city so he invited the Sabine people to a party – and captured all their women for his men to marry. Another problem solved.

In the end Romulus disappeared in a storm – and became a god!

165

Believe all that and you need a Roman woodpecker to peck some sense into your wooden head! But...

Did you know...?

The story of Romulus and Remus was *not* the story the Romans usually told their children about the making of Rome. The Romans liked to believe that the first Romans came from near Greece, after the battle of Troy.

You remember that tale? Where the Trojans were beaten by a wooden horse full of Greek soldiers (and probably a few Greek woodpeckers)? Well, some Trojans escaped. They were led into Italy by the hero, Aeneas, and they ended up starting the towns that became Rome.

The Romans simply invented a list of kings and said, 'This is our history!' Which just goes to show – you can never trust a history book. Except a *Horrible Histories* book, of course.

The rotten republic

After the Romans threw out King Tarquin in 510 BC they really began spreading out around the world. Of course the people the Romans conquered didn't *want* to be conquered. There were lots of bloody battles and bad feelings. The Romans usually won because they were more ruthless than their enemies. They even practised being bloodthirsty by slaughtering people in Rome – for fun.

Rotten republic timeline

390 BC The Gauls (from France) invade Rome and wreck most of the houses and temples. So the Romans build a city wall. Sensible. It will mark the boundary for the next 600 years.

295 BC Decius Mus wins a battle for the Romans that makes them lords of Italy. Now there's just the rest of the world to go out and grab.

264–231 BC Rome at war against Carthage (North Africa). Romans need to learn how to fight at sea as well as on land.

218 BC Rome at war with Carthage again – they are stuffed by Hannibal at Trasimene and then Cannae. In 202 BC they finally beat Hannibal. Who can stop them now?

146 BC The Romans destroy the Greek city of Corinth and destroy the ancient Greek fighting spirit. Glorious Greece becomes part of rotten Rome. The Mediterranean Sea is starting to look like a Roman lake – they own everything around it.

132 BC Tiberius Gracchus tries to change the way Rome is run – take power from the rich and give land to the poor. The rich are not happy so they murder Gracchus. Murdering Roman leaders will now become a Roman hobby. Gracchus' brother

167

fails with the same plan and kills himself – another Roman hobby.

82 BC Romans are squabbling among themselves. Sulla marches in with an army, massacres anyone who is against him, and takes over as a dictator. The beginning of the end for the republic.

73 BC Gladiators revolt, led by super Spartacus, and rampage around Italy. But they never manage to capture Rome. They are finally defeated and crucified. Roman Crassus is the hero and becomes the new top Roman with General Pompey.

55 BC Superstar general Julius Caesar smashes Gaul and crosses into Germany and Britain. He's a great man, popular with the people. Then Crassus dies in battle with the Parthians. That leaves just Julius and Pompey as top dogs.

49 BC Pompey (back in Rome) tells Julius Caesar (up in Gaul), 'I will let you help me rule Rome – *if* you come back and leave your army behind.' Julius doesn't trust him. He refuses to come quietly and arrives in Rome with his army. Pompey runs away. It is the start of 19 years of Romans fighting Romans.

46 BC Julius Caesar wins power and has a party – a death party. Hundreds of gladiator fights and animal hunts in the arena. He says they are funeral fights, in memory of his daughter – though she died *eight years* earlier! But republics only work when people agree: 'Winners rule OK'. The Roman republic fell apart because there were too many *really* bad losers who said: 'Winners die OK'. Losers turned into rebels, killed the winners and became the winners. So other losers killed the new winners … and, oh, you can see how it goes on…

44 BC Caesar's just too powerful. He is stabbed to death by worried enemies. Caesar's nephew Octavian and his old friend Mark Antony will share power for a while but sooner or later they will fight one another, won't they?

31 BC Octavian declares war on Mark Antony's girlfriend Cleopatra, Queen of Egypt. Narked Mark has to fight for her. He's beaten and kills himself. Octavian top dog now and…

27 BC …Rome (which hates having a king) makes Octavian 'Emperor'. He changes his name to 'Augustus'. End of the 'republic' – but really it's been finished for 50 years – and start of the 'empire'.

Super superstitions and quaint customs

The Romans had dozens of gods. You've probably had to learn some of them in school and know the usual boring ones: Neptune – god of the sea, Jupiter – chief god … that sort of thing. But there were Roman gods that even your teacher has never heard of. It may be useful to call on one of these gods at the right moment! These may look weird, wacky and made-up, but they are true…

Horrible Histories **top five gods and goddesses**

AT NUMBER 5 WE HAVE... CORDEA-GODDESS OF HINGES

AND AT NUMBER 4 WE HAVE... PENATES-GOD OF CUPBOARDS

AT NUMBER 3 WE HAVE... ROBIGUS-GOD OF MILDEW (THAT NASTY MOULD THAT GROWS IN DAMP PLACES)

IN AT NUMBER 2 WE HAVE... TERMINUS-GOD OF BOUNDARIES

AND AT NUMBER 1 WE HAVE THE GODDESS FURRINA!

Furrina's festival was celebrated every 25 July, but by 100 BC no one could remember what she was goddess of!

So there you have it! On 25 July let's all have a party. A party for anything you like, and Furrina can be your goddess! Have a party for your hamster – Furrina can be the goddess of furry things. Have a party for the end of term – Furrina is the goddess of school holidays! Furrina is the greatest goddess of all because she's the goddess of whatever you want her to be!

Act like a Roman

Fancy being a Roman priest? Then here's what you do…

Whipping people was part of a ceremony called the 'Lupercalia' – on 15 February each year. This would persuade the gods to bring you good crops and large herds of animals the following summer. Sometimes the Romans sacrificed dogs at the Lupercalia.

Did you know…?
In October the winning horse in a chariot race was sacrificed. The tail, dripping blood, was used to bless the crops. Different districts of Rome had a competition to see which one could have the biggest prize – the horse's head.

Awesome augury
'Augury' was the Roman name for fortune-telling – looking into the future. The Romans were so superstitious they had an augury 'kit' that they took with them into battle.

You may want to look into the future yourself. If so then why not try the Roman augury method. This will allow you to…

- Check your exam results before you even take the tests. (See if it's worth even going to school!)
- Find out if it's a good time to ask your parents for a pocket-money rise. (Or will you have to wash Dad's car … again?)

172

• See if your football team will win on Saturday. (Or should you save your ticket money and stay in bed?)

Here's how to augur...

Augur away

You need:
Sacred chickens. (Chickens from your local butcher aren't good enough. They have to be living chickens. If they're not holy chickens then take them to your local temple and have the vicar sprinkle them with holy water.)
Some cake with seeds on top.

To augur:
1 Feed small pieces of the cake to the sacred chickens.
2 Watch the chickens eat the cake.

The meaning:
If the chickens eat the cake and bits of seed fall out of their beaks then this is a good sign. Today whatever you do will be lucky.

But if the chickens refuse to eat the cake then this is a bad sign. Do not go into battle/school/hysterics. Stay in bed and pray the gods don't send a thunderbolt to get you while you are lying there.

Of course, the Romans knew that the sacred chickens were messengers of the gods. Roman admiral Claudius Pulcher saw chickens refuse to eat before a sea battle with Carthage.

He threw the chickens overboard saying he didn't believe their message of doom, but the chickens had the last laugh – or at least the last cluck. The Romans lost 93 ships and the battle.

Wonderful weddings

Romans often used fortune-telling as part of their wedding ceremonies. A posh Roman service included prayers and a bloodless sacrifice (roasting a cabbage and offering it to a god). Guests would also eat holy bread, and the bride and groom would sit in two chairs that were tied together and covered in lamb-skin.

What other way could you be married in ancient Rome – especially if you weren't posh and couldn't afford the holy bread and priests and all that?

a) Just agreeing, 'We are married … OK?'.

b) Living together for a year – so long as the wife isn't away from home for more than three days.

c) Agreeing to be married in front of five people and someone holding a pair of scales.

Answer: All of them.

Batty beliefs

Would you walk under a ladder? A lot of people today believe that will bring them bad luck. (It would if the ladder was attached to a fire-engine speeding towards you at 60 miles an hour.) Here are a few strange superstitions – but which did Romans believe? Answer true or false…

1 It is bad luck to enter a house left-foot first.
2 Sausages should be banned.
3 It is lucky to have a cow on the roof of your house.

4 Women should comb their hair with the spear of a dead man for luck.
5 Dead people can become ghosts.
6 If a man dreams of being a gladiator he will marry a rich woman.
7 The birthday of Emperor Tiberius' sister-in-law is a lucky day in Rome.
8 Animals should only be sacrificed after they ask for it.
9 Crows are lucky.
10 A lightning strike is caused by angry gods so you should sacrifice four enemies to keep the gods happy.

Answers:

1 True. Rich Romans put a servant at the door to make sure everyone entered right-foot first. That's where we get the name 'footman' for a servant.

2 True. Sausages were banned in Rome by Emperor Constantine. They were eaten at barbarian festivals and Constantine didn't want Romans mixed up with those dreadful people.

3 False. They believed it was *un*lucky. In 191 BC, two cows climbed on to the roof of a Roman house. The city priests said this was a bad sign. They ordered the cattle to be burned alive and their ashes to be scattered on the River Tiber.

4 True. The man should have been killed in the arena – the fresher the better.

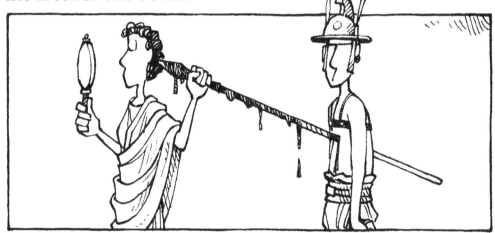

5 True. A murdered person would haunt the world, hoping to take revenge on their murderer.

6 True. The bad news is the rich woman you married would be sly and big-headed.

7 False. Tiberius hated Agrippina and sent her to Pandataria Island where she starved herself to death. The Emperor made her birthday one of Rome's days of bad luck.

8 True. The animal that went for the chop had to show it wanted to die. How? By stretching its neck out for the axe. Could the Romans cheat and get the animal to stretch its neck out? You bet!

9 False. Crows were an unlucky sign. Ruthless Roman rebel Sejanus was surrounded by cawing crows that then went off to settle on the prison roof. Sejanus should have seen it as a sign. Shortly after he was arrested and executed. He was surprised by the arrest. But the crows had tried to warn him!

10 True. In 228 BC the lightning scared the Romans gathered in the forum and a fortune teller said there was only one way to stop it happening again – sacrifice two couples of enemy tribespeople. They buried two Celts and two Greeks alive under the forum. They could still be there to this day!

Cruel curses

The Romans believed you could curse your enemies and bring them bad luck. It may be true! Why not try it? Here's what to do…

1 Write down the name of a dead person – their ghost will do the dirty work.
2 Write down who you want to curse.
3 Write down what you want to happen.
Here is an example…

Dear Julius Caesar,
Please curse Mrs Popplewick of 5 Willow Way, Walberswick, for telling my mum I bounced my football off her nice clean car. I had to clean the whole car again thanks to pooey Popplewick. May the hair on her chin turn into a big bushy beard! Thank you, Mr Caesar.

Henry Hooligan

4 Take your curse to the nearest well and drop it down.
5 Wait and see what happens.

178

Grim ghosts

When Emperor Caligula died his body was burned in his garden … but not completely. What was left was buried, but the garden became haunted. Caligula's sisters had the remains dug up and burned to complete ashes. The ghost never returned.

That was just one of many ghost stories the Romans told. A Roman called Pliny wrote a letter in which he told another ghost story. A ghost told his friend, Athenodorus, where to find his corpse…

ATHENODORUS ROSE FROM HIS BED AND WENT OUT OF THE DOOR. THE GARDEN WAS LIT BY A HALF MOON AND THE GHOSTLY SHAPE WAS CLEARER THERE. IT WAS THE SHAPE OF A SMALL MAN AND HIS HEAD SEEMED TO DRIP BLOOD. THE HIDEOUS CREATURE POINTED TO A SPOT BETWEEN THE WALL AND THE SUNDIAL AND SAID, 'DIG THERE AND FIND MY MURDERED BODY. GIVE ME A TRUE ROMAN BURIAL SO MY SPIRIT MAY REST.'

ATHENODORUS MOVED TOWARDS THE SPOT AND THE GHOSTLY FIGURE VANISHED. NEXT MORNING HE HAD SLAVES DIG WHERE THE GHOST TOLD HIM AND THEY CAME ACROSS A BODY IN A BLOOD-STAINED SHEET. IT WAS ALMOST ROTTED TO A SKELETON. THEY RAISED IT AND TOOK IT OUTSIDE OF THE CITY TO A CEMETERY AND GAVE IT A BURIAL. SINCE THAT DAY ATHENODORUS HAS NOT BEEN TROUBLED BY THE GHOST.

You may not believe the ghost story, but most Romans would have believed it. For the Romans, it was important to bury friends properly. Criminals could be torn apart in the arena by wild animals, but that was only part of their punishment. The other part was to have their corpses dumped without a funeral, which meant they would *never* get to the Roman heaven. Maybe those thousands of victims are still wandering the Earth, crying, 'Help! Help! I've been eaten by a crocodile!' Spooky or what?

Heavenly horrors

The Romans believed that after you died you went to a place called the Underworld. You crossed the River Styx on a ferry and went to a happier place. But if your corpse hadn't been properly buried then the ferryman, Charon, would not let you cross. Your corpse just lay on the banks of the river till dogs came to eat it.

A Roman writer told a story of a man who went to the Underworld and saw the unburied dead scattered around. The 'Furies' – vicious 'avenging angels' – hung around there and enjoyed the hideous sights:

On the shores of Ugliness there was a huge plain, covered with corpses that had suffered dreadful deaths. Some had been beheaded and some crucified. Pitiful bodies stood there with their throats freshly cut. The Furies were laughing at the misery of the victims. There was a sickening smell of blood.

Gory Gladiators

Gladiators were men (and sometimes women) who fought in front of an audience – a bit like some footballers today. But footballers aren't given swords and spears and nets to fight with. Though it's a nice idea…

Most gladiator fights stopped when one fighter was too wounded or exhausted to go on. But some of the fights went on till one of the gladiators was dead. Where on earth did the Romans get this gruesome idea from?

Like a lot of their ideas, it was probably pinched. (The Romans pinched their religion, letters and writing, and theatre from the Greeks, for example. They even stole complete Greek temples and shipped them over to Rome.)

They nicked the public-killing idea from the Etruscan people who once ruled the Romans. These Etruscans lived just to the north and ruled Rome in the early days. The Etruscans could be pretty nasty. In 356 BC they sacrificed 307 Roman prisoners in the centre of the city. (And the Etruscans possibly 'borrowed' *their* ideas from the Greeks.)

This gladiator thing all started at funerals. Nowadays a funeral means a few words from the vicar followed by tea and sandwiches. The Etruscan funerals didn't have tea or sandwiches – they just murdered one of their enemies over the grave. It was revenge, and it was a gift to the dead man.

181

If the dead man *was* happy in heaven then he wouldn't come back to haunt the living. So funeral killers were the first ghost-busters.

But, did you know that sometimes the Etruscans killed a puppet instead of a living human?

Then the Etruscans thought of a new idea – it was much more exciting. Take TWO prisoners (or slaves or criminals) and let them fight each other at the grave. Call them 'gladiators'. The loser becomes the sacrifice to the dead person.

To make the contest even more exciting the gladiators were trained to fight in special gladiator schools – watching skilled fighters was more interesting than watching two men with swords just chop at one another.

Romans began to ask for gladiator fights *before* they died.

One man, Sestillius, wrote in his will…

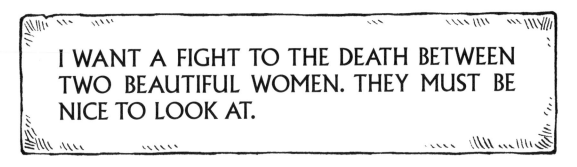

I WANT A FIGHT TO THE DEATH BETWEEN TWO BEAUTIFUL WOMEN. THEY MUST BE NICE TO LOOK AT.

Another, Messinus, wrote a will which said…

In life I loved the company of two young slaves, Marcus and Tarquin. I want them to fight to the death over my grave.

GEE THANKS, BOSS

Messinus *didn't* get his wish. The Romans felt sorry for the boys and stopped it.

But the Romans weren't always so kind. In Pollentia a man was going to be buried *without* a gladiator fight at the funeral. So the people of the town stopped the funeral and wouldn't let the family bury him till they had paid for a gladiator fight. Nasty. And things got nastier…

In the year 264 BC, a Roman called Brutus Pera had *three* gladiator fights at his funeral. And they were moved out of the graveyard and into the cattle market so everyone could get a good view. The contests became bigger and bigger.

By 216 BC there were 22 fights going on at a single funeral.

In 174 BC, a chap called Flamininus had a great funeral for his dead dad: it went on for three days and involved 74 gladiators. Would you do that for your dad?

Killer Colosseum

At first gladiator games were held in any open spaces – marketplaces, forums or fields. But by around 100 BC people were building special arenas. The greatest killing ground of all was the Colosseum in Rome. It held 50,000 people and it was opened in AD 80.

Easy question: Why was it called the 'Colosseum'?

Answer: Because it was built near the colossal statue of Emperor Nero.

Very hard question: Why were its large columns *cemented* together? They were supposed to be pinned with big iron pins but…

a) Romans kept pinching the pins.

b) The pins went rusty and the building almost fell down before it was finished.

c) The gladiators needed the pins to make enough swords to slaughter all the animals.

Answer: **a)** You can't trust anyone, can you?

185

Did you know…?

The Colosseum was the size of a modern football stadium – and that was *small*! The Circus Maximus was *twelve* times bigger than the Colosseum, and would hold a quarter of a million people – that's a quarter of all the people in Rome.

The Romans packed the Circus Maximus to watch chariot races. It was more popular than the Colosseum because men and women could sit together there – that wasn't allowed in the Colosseum.

Crushing defeat

The Colosseum was fairly safe because it was built of stone. But some earlier arenas were definitely *not* safe – or as safe as a hedgehog on a motorway. A writer called Tacitus described one…

At Fidenae there was an accident that killed as many as a great war. It began and ended in a moment. An ex-slave, Atilius, built an arena for gladiator shows. But he didn't build it on solid ground and he didn't fasten the wooden platforms together very firmly. He only built it to make some easy money. Fans flocked in – men and women of all ages – because there had been very few good shows in the reign of Emperor Tiberius. The packed building collapsed, inwards and outwards, crushing or smothering a huge crowd.

Tacitus went on to say the dead were the lucky ones – it was worse for the mangled fans who knew their loved ones were trapped somewhere in the mess of wood and bodies.

In the daytime they could see them – at night they could hear their screams and moans. When the ruins were cleared people rushed in to kiss and hug the corpses of their families. They even argued over bodies that were so smashed they weren't sure whose they were. Fifty thousand were killed or injured.

The crowds had rushed in to see blood in the arena, and they certainly saw it.

Emperor Caligula did *not* have a big arena collapse in his time. He said…

What a shame – it must be interesting to watch!

Not from the bottom of the heap, Caligula.

Did you know…?
Games were usually fought on sand. But emperors Caligula and Nero liked coloured dust instead. They mixed white and greenish-blue dust with red dust. A pretty place to die.

Scrapping spectators

One of the first arenas was built in Pompeii in around 80 BC. It held 20,000 people – a lot for a fairly small town. How did they fill it? With people from other towns in the region. And that's how the trouble started.

People came in from the town of Nuceria – and the people of Nuceria hated the people of Pompeii, just like some rival football fans still do today. The Nucerians wrote nasty graffiti on the walls of Pompeii and probably enjoyed threatening their rivals. Tacitus described what happened next…

It was the sort of deadly riot that you could still imagine happening at a football ground today, sadly. In Rome the emperor was horrified to hear what had happened. What would *you* do if you were emperor after such a murderous riot?

a) Invite the people of Pompeii and Nuceria to fight in Rome.

b) Ban all games in Pompeii for ten years.

c) Have the Pompeii arena pulled down.

Answer: The shocked emperor did b).

Prezzies for the plebs

The posh people in Rome were the 'patricians'; the workers were the 'plebeians' (or plebs for short). The patricians may have ruled the country, but they needed to keep the plebs happy. So the patricians gave the plebs the bloody arena games, they gave them food and they gave them gifts. The rich often gave out gifts at New Year.

In Roman Alexandria a rich man paraded a wagon through the streets with a model of a cave built on it. Doves were released from the cave with long ribbons tied to their feet. The poor could grab a ribbon to catch a dove – and eat it!

The greatest of the gift-givers was usually the emperor. At the arena some would give out lottery tickets with prizes for the lucky ones. Emperor Elagabalus gave out slips of paper with the prizes written on them…

There were slaves and even houses to be won. No wonder people were trampled to death as they scrambled to get one of Elagabalus' bits of paper.

But Elagabalus had a nasty sense of humour. Some of the prizes were *not* what you'd like to win in your school raffle.

Lies my teacher told

Teachers learn from other teachers and from books. But sometimes they get their facts wrong because some books are wrong. But, as this is a *Horrible Histories* book, you can at last hear the truth.

1 Gladiator deaths

Gladiators fought to the death

Oh no they didn't. Not all of them anyway.

Proper gladiators cost a lot of money to feed and train. Posh Romans paid the bills and put on gladiator shows for the poor Romans. In return, the poor Romans voted for them. No one would spend all that money to see it wasted with a few short, sharp chops. In fact, the top gladiators fought like today's boxers – the crowds loved watching their skill and betting on who would win. Those top gladiators lived to fight again.

Roman noble Cicero wrote to a friend...

What fine gladiators you have bought. If you had rented them out you could have got your money back on just those two shows.

So, gladiators were groups of entertainers, bought by the rich for free shows or to be hired out. Gladiators were *not* cheap slaves to be wasted in the arena.

Criminals *were* sent in to the arena to fight till they died. They dressed like gladiators but the Romans knew they were not the real thing. Those criminals (called 'noxii') gave the Romans all the blood and death they wanted. Prisoners of war were also sent to the arena just to be slaughtered.

Noxii were badly trained, and had little chance of winning. Even if they did win they fought on until someone beat them. But the real gladiators fought for years and many won their freedom after giving the crowds lots of fighting fun. Emperor Tiberius even complained:

I had to pay one old, free gladiator a thousand gold pieces to get him back into the arena!

Did you know…?

Emperor Caligula liked to have people executed and then sell off all they had owned. Sometimes Caligula held an auction and he did the selling. If you wanted to buy something you just had to nod your head. One old senator, Aponius, fell asleep and his head kept nodding. When he woke up he found he had bought 13 gladiators … and they cost him 90,000 gold pieces!

2 Gladiator salute

Gladiators who entered the arena cried to the emperor:

'We who are about to die salute you'

Oh no they didn't. This happened only *once*. And the dying men were *not* gladiators. They were criminals who were put in a mock sea battle. They had to kill each other to entertain Emperor Claudius. They cried out 'We salute you' in the hope that the Emperor would spare their lives. He said, 'Get on with it.'

At first they refused to fight. The Emperor threatened them: 'Fight or my guards will burn and hack you to death!' Then they tried to fight without hurting each other too much. Again they were told to fight properly or die.

The criminals began to really fight. The Emperor enjoyed it and spared the lives of the ones who survived.

Glad-iator to meet you

The Roman poet Ovid said the arena was a very good place to meet women. How can you chat one up? Just turn to them and ask…

These programmes were sold in the streets and in the arenas – just like programmes at football matches today. To be honest, you didn't have to have a printed programme.

The programme was usually the same…

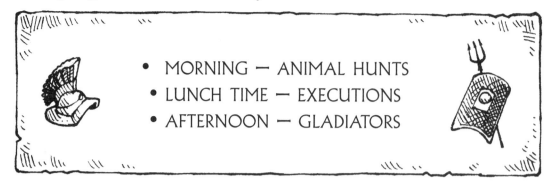

- MORNING — ANIMAL HUNTS
- LUNCH TIME — EXECUTIONS
- AFTERNOON — GLADIATORS

Plus there were heralds who entered the arena and shouted out the names of the fighters or the criminals, and servants carrying banners into the arena with the names on.

There were also adverts for the arena games painted by roadsides. If there wasn't a wall handy then the painter would paint the latest gladiator news on a gravestone!

Fighting fellers

There were several types of gladiators – it would be boring if they were all dressed and armed the same way. Here are the main ones:

ANDABATAE

Fought blindfolded – very funny for the audience.

DIMACHERI

Fought with two swords – slick slicers.

RETIARII

Fought with nets and a trident – a bit fishy that.

HOPLOMACHI

Fought in a suit of armour – hot work.

LAQUEATORES

Fought with a rope – no noose was bad news for them.

SECUTORES

Fought with sword and shield – they were lucky ones.

SAGITTARII
Fought with bows and arrows – hoping for an arrow escape.

BESTIARII
Fought with anything against wild animals – beastly.

BUT one sort of gladiator you won't hear about in school books were the 'scissores'. The word means 'carvers'. Why will you not see a picture of 'scissores' in your school books?

a) They didn't exist (I just made them up).

b) 'Scissores' were dressmakers who fought with scissors in the street, not the arena.

c) No one knows anything about them except for their name.

Answer: **c)** The name 'scissores' is carved on a stone in a list of gladiators. But no one knows what they did. So here, for the first time, is an image of what we think this fiendish fighter may have looked like…

Freedom fighters

Most gladiators were slaves, but some freemen chose to become gladiators. If they did well they could retire rich. Gladiator Publius Ostorius was a freeman and had 51 fights.

But he had to give up his freedom. He had to sign a contract before he entered gladiator school. Would you sign this for the pleasure of going to school…?

I AGREE TO LET MY MASTERS…
- BURN ME WITH FIRE
- FASTEN ME WITH CHAINS
- WHIP ME WITH RODS
- KILL ME WITH STEEL

AURELIUS TWITTUS

The only way out was to buy yourself out. One Roman story tells of a girl who bought her brother out of gladiator school – but he went back. So she bought him out again … and again … and again. In the end she waited till he was asleep and cut off his thumb so he could never hold a sword and never fight again. The gladiator wanted revenge in court…

I WANT HER THUMB CUT OFF TOO

Wild women

Women sometimes fought as gladiators. But many men were shocked at the idea. The Roman poet Juvenal wrote a very nasty poem about female gladiators. He said they were not only a disgrace to their husbands – they were also just a joke as fighters…

The Gorgeous Gladiators by Juvenal

See how she slashes at dummies of wood,
As she trains for the fighting, she is simply no good.
See how the helmet just weighs down her head,
Though there's really no chance that she'll end up plain dead.
Why does she fight? Does she think she's a bloke?
Her husband should tell her she looks like a joke.
The bandages thick make her legs look like trees,
We laugh when she rests as she squats down and pees.
Panting and groaning with sweat on her face,
She only brings women pure shame and disgrace.

In 200 AD, Emperor Septimius Severus agreed with Juvenal. He banned women from fighting in the arena … but, he said, it was still OK to throw them in to be torn apart by wild animals, of course.

Cheating chaps

Gladiators were supposed to fight hard and put on a good show for the audience. But one group shocked Emperor Caligula when they refused to fight. Here's what happened…

A GROUP OF RETIARII ENTERED THE ARENA...

THEN THEIR OPPONENTS, SECUTORES, ENTERED...

Caligula called it 'murder' and he probably had the Retiarii executed anyway. But at least they must have had a bit of a chuckle before they died!

A dreadful way to die

Not all criminals wanted to die in front of a screaming crowd of Romans. Some killed themselves before they entered the arena. But that wasn't easy because criminals sentenced to fight to the death were guarded day and night. The only time they had to themselves was in the toilet.

In the toilet there were sticks with sponges on the end. These were dipped in water and used instead of toilet paper – get the picture? Everyone used the same sponges and rinsed them after they used them.

A German prisoner of war was due to go in the arena and said, 'I want to use the toilet before I go in.' The guard allowed him to go.

The German took the toilet sponge and pushed it down his throat till the sharp stick had killed him.

Other criminals were known to kill themselves by leaning over the side of the cart that took them to the games. If they could stick their head in the spokes of the cartwheel it would crush their skull as it turned. Around AD 390, 29 Saxons strangled each other rather than fight.

Bopped bodies

It was no use faking a fight. If you were meant to die in the arena the Romans made sure you did. How? Two men came into the arena after your fight. One was dressed in a tight

200

tunic, wore soft leather boots and a mask that gave him the nose of a hawk. He carried a big hammer.

In front of Dis was another man with wings on his helmet and carrying a red-hot poker…

Mercury stuck his red-hot poker into you to make sure you weren't just pretending to be dead, then Dis made absolutely sure by smashing you very hard on the forehead. Then slaves came and carried you off on a stretcher. It was a bit like a football match today … at least that very small bit with the stretcher is.

But if you were a criminal who had been executed in the arena then hooks were stuck in your body and you were dragged out – and that doesn't happen to footballers today. (Not even footballers in Rome.)

Ruthless Roman army

The Romans won a lot of fights. Teacher tells you they had...

DISCIPLINE! THE ROMAN SOLDIERS DID WHAT THEY WERE TOLD! WHAT DID THEY DO, DEREK?

PLEASE, SIR, WHAT THEY WERE TOLD, SIR!

And they had good stabbing swords and armour and ... zzzz! Excuse us while we fall asleep. Never mind the armour and the weapons. What you really want to know is that they were *ruthless*. They were nasty, cruel and vicious. *That's* why they won.

If you are a soldier and you surrender, you might expect your enemy to spare your life. Not if the enemy was a Roman. And the Romans didn't just kill their prisoners – they took them back to Rome and killed them in the city centre so the rest of the Romans could watch.

Doggy disaster

When the Romans captured New Carthage in Spain in 202 BC their general, Scipio, gave the order...

Kill everyone you meet.

The soldiers did more than that – they cut the legs off animals and chopped dogs in two. Picture it: chopped chows to the left, poodle pieces to the right and halved hounds h'everywhere.

Evil to enemies

In AD 70, the Romans wanted to capture Jerusalem but the Jewish defenders refused to surrender. The Romans had thousands of Jewish prisoners. Every day the Romans crucified 500 of those prisoners outside the walls of the city so their friends could watch them die in agony. And this went on for several months!

If a Roman soldier was really kind he'd break the legs of the victim nailed to the cross – that way the crucified person would die in a couple of hours. But the Roman soldiers could often be extra cruel to people they didn't like and they could keep them alive on the cross for two or three days so the suffering went on and on.

Death for deserters

If you ran away from a battle then the Romans would probably execute you. But if your whole legion ran away they couldn't execute you *all*, could they? Sometimes.

- In AD 214, 370 men were thrown from the Tarpeian Rock in Rome for deserting.
- In that year a Roman commander captured 2,000 deserters in Sicily and beheaded every one.

- In 146 BC, cruel General Scipio crucified runaways from his army.
- But cruellest of all, in 167 BC, the Roman leader Lucius Aemilius Paullus laid a group of deserters down on the ground – and had them *trampled by elephants*.

More often, a troop of cowards were 'decimated' – which meant having one soldier in every ten killed. The survivors were sent back into battle. Emperor Augustus made the nine 'lucky' soldiers club their 'unlucky' friend to death.

Soldiers didn't even have to run away to get this treatment. Crassus had 500 soldiers out of 5,000 decimated when their only 'crime' was to lose in battle to Spartacus and his gladiator rebels. Don't blame the general – blame the soldiers.

Imagine decimating football teams if they lost!

Ruthless to rebels

Some Roman soldiers who rebelled against Rome were executed in an odd way. In 270 BC over 300 troops rebelled and were marched back to Rome. They were tied to stakes and whipped till they were half dead. Then they were finished off by having the backs of their necks chopped with an axe. They weren't beheaded completely – maybe that would leave too many bits to pick up?

Whips for winners

Romans loved a winner. If a general's army killed 5,000 of the enemy in battle, he was given a parade through Rome. The men got their share of the captured loot and marched to the temple of Jupiter. Jupiter's statue has a red face – and the Roman general's face was painted red to match. (That must have looked dreadful with the purple and gold robes he was given for the day.) Then, to remind him not to get too big-headed, there was a whip attached to his chariot – that's what Rome would use on him if he misbehaved. Just to round off the party a defeated enemy general was put to death. Nice.

Tricky tactics

The Roman army won a lot of wars because they were just too clever for the enemy. In 396 BC they had been trying for ten years to get into the city of Veii, north of Rome, where their Etruscan enemies were holding out. At last General Furius Camillus came up with a cunning plot to enter the city. If he'd written a report back to the senate it may have looked like this...

SIRS,

VEII IS TAKEN. FOR YEARS WE HAVE FAILED TO ATTACK UP THE HILL TO THE CITY, SO I DECIDED TO DIG THROUGH THE HILL. MY MEN DUG A TUNNEL RIGHT UP TO THEIR TEMPLE OF JUNO. WE COULD HEAR THEIR KING OFFERING A SACRIFICE.

WE BROKE THROUGH AND AFTER FIERCE FIGHTING WE OVERCAME THE PEOPLE OF VEII. WOMEN AND SLAVES WERE HURLING STONES DOWN ON OUR MEN FROM THE ROOFTOPS. WE SET FIRE TO THE HOUSES AND THEY WERE BURNED ALIVE FOR THEIR CHEEK.

OUR VICTORIOUS TROOPS ARE RETURNING TO ROME. I LOOK FORWARD TO A GLORIOUS WELCOME.

FURIUS CAMILLIUS

But the reply was not at all what he expected.

FURIUS CAMILLUS,
REPORTS HAVE REACHED US THAT THERE WAS GREAT WEALTH IN VEII AND THAT YOU HAVE TAKEN A LARGE SHARE OF IT FOR YOURSELF. AS YOU KNOW, ALL LOOT COMES TO ROME FIRST. THE SENATE HAS DECIDED TODAY TO HAVE YOU EXILED.

ALL GOOD WISHES,

SECRETARY TO THE SENATE

Poor old Furius! (A lot of other popular history books would say, 'Bet he was furious!' But this is a *Horrible Histories* book and we don't have awful jokes like that … much.) Furius had the last laugh, though. When the Gauls attacked, in 390 BC, the Romans had to call him back to help them.

Evil enemies

Why were the Romans so ruthless? Maybe they had to be, because their enemies could be pretty rotten to Romans when the Romans lost. And the Romans didn't always win.

Mind you, when they lost it wasn't always the savage enemies that beat them – sometimes it was their own stupid leaders! In 217 BC Hannibal's army from Carthage was helped by the weather – and by a very careless Roman general…

THE ROMAN TIMES

HORRIBLE HANNIBAL LASHES LEGIONS

Harmful Hannibal

The Roman army has suffered a dreadful defeat at the hands of Hannibal and his Carthage cut-throats. Hannibal was being chased right back to Carthage by our bold boys and hid in the hills above Lake Trasimene. He knew the Romans were on his tail and he planned an awful ambush.

Roman general Flaminius led his legions along the shore of the lake but fat-head Flaminius didn't send scouts on ahead. So he had no idea what was waiting round the corner.

The crafty Carthage men were helped by a foul fog that

floated over the lake and hid Hannibal's army. When they rushed down from the hills our legions were driven into the lake. Many of our soggy soldiers sank and drowned. We have lost four legions and Hannibal is now heading for Rome itself.

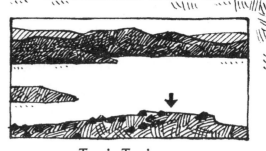

Tragic Trasimene

It's a bad day for the Roman people – and we all know who to blame.

Worse was still to come. The Romans lost the next big battle with Hannibal at Cannae in 216 BC. Hannibal's African army slaughtered them. But he never went on to take the city of Rome. In the end, the Romans raised new armies, defeated Carthage and destroyed the city completely – they even sowed the fields with salt so nothing could grow there.

Burning Sulla

The Romans believed it was best to bury their dead heroes in graves. Then word reached Rome that their enemies were digging up the corpses and scattering them around. So the Roman general Sulla started a new fashion – cremation...

WHEN I DIE I DON'T WANT PEOPLE DIGGING ME UP IN REVENGE. BURN MY BODY PLEASE

He died in 78 BC and they followed his wishes so he became the first important Roman to be cremated.

Nasty for Numidia

The Roman armies really enjoyed taking captured enemies back to Rome and showing them to the Roman people. Enemy leaders were flogged then dragged with nooses around their necks to the forum. Then they were executed and that was an excuse for the Romans to have lots of parties.

Numidia in North Africa was ruled by Jugurtha – who thought he was better than the Romans. He murdered his enemies, who happened to be friends of the Romans, and the Romans were not very pleased with him. In 110 BC he drove the Romans out of Numidia. It was time for them to get ruthless.

In 105 BC the Romans invited him to Rome to explain himself to the senate – a bit like you being called to see the head teacher! (Why was Jugurtha daft enough to go to Rome? Because his wife's dad said he would be safe.)

Jugurtha said…

The senate said, 'Fine! But, before you go, we have a parade arranged for you.'

Then the ruthless Romans led Jugurtha through the streets of Rome. But there was a nasty surprise waiting for him at the end of the parade. His clothes and jewels were torn off him, and when his ear-ring was torn off it took half his ear with it. Then Jugurtha was thrown into a cold prison cell. The shock drove him mad and he died after six days from cold and starvation.

Laugh with the lions

When the Megarians from Greece attacked the Roman army of Julius Caesar they used a secret weapon – lions that had been trained to eat victims in the arenas.

The Megarians set the lions on to the Romans – but the lions turned round and attacked the Megarians instead! (Maybe Megarians taste better than Romans!) The Roman soldiers must have had a bit of a laugh that day.

Cut-throat Celts?

The Celts liked to collect the heads of their enemies. They put them on show and boasted about how they had killed them. But did you know that it wasn't only the Celts who had this horrible hobby. The Romans soon copied the cruel Celt collectors…

- From 87 BC the Romans were quite keen on collecting heads. A top Roman official, Consul Octavius, was beheaded that year and his head shown in the forum. Many senator heads followed and the Romans became head-hunters, carrying the heads of defeated enemies back to Rome.

- In 43 BC Roman troops cut off the head of Trebonius who was one of Caesar's murderers. They threw and kicked the head across the pavements till it was smashed to pieces.

- Old Galba was emperor for just nine months before he was assassinated in Rome. His head was carried round the city on the end of a spear. His servant rescued it and buried it with his body.

- Galba's supporters got the head treatment, too. The Greek historian Plutarch wrote…

> The dead bodies of Galba's friends were scattered all over the forum. And, as for their heads, when the new emperor's army had no more use for them, that of Piso was given to his wife. That of Vinius was sold to his daughter.

Sold? To his daughter? How much would you give for your dad's dead head?

Super Spartacus

In 73 BC a gladiator called Spartacus led a rebellion in Rome. Who was he? He was from Thrace (which is called Bulgaria now) and originally he'd joined the Roman army. Then he'd deserted and become an outlaw. When he was captured he was forced to be a gladiator. He was so good he became a gladiator teacher.

Then he decided to go home and lead all his gladiator friends to freedom. Now, gladiators practised with wooden swords – they weren't allowed to use real swords until they went into the arena. So how did they make their escape past the Roman soldiers guarding them?

a) They went to the gladiator kitchens and pinched the knives.

b) They made their wooden swords really sharp and splintered the guards to death.

c) They put poison on the tips of their wooden swords and stabbed the guards.

Answer: **a)** Once they'd cut a few Roman soldiers' throats, of course, they could then steal the Roman weapons.

212

Spartacus' plot

Spartacus camped in the crater of the volcano Vesuvius – which, of course, was not erupting at the time. There was one easy path to the top of Vesuvius but around the other three sides there were cliffs. The Romans, led by Claudius Glaber, were happy...

All the Romans had to do was march up the path and attack the rebel gladiators.

If you were Spartacus, what would you do? (Clue: vines are very tough climbing plants with branches like rope.) Well? Are you as clever as Spartacus?

Here's what he did:

- His men cut the vines and made them into long ladders.
- They threw the ladders over the cliffs and all but one of them climbed out of the crater.
- The last man threw his weapon down and then climbed down himself.
- The gladiators walked round to the bottom of the one path so they came at the Romans from behind – where the Romans weren't expecting them.
- The gladiators attacked the Romans, beat them and captured their camp and their weapons.

213

Plutarch wrote…

> And now Spartacus was joined by farmers and shepherds of those parts, all tough men and fast on their feet. Some of these were armed as soldiers and some were used as spies.

Of course, the weapons came from the careless Romans. Spartacus had a real army now, not just a bunch of bandits. Big mistake, Claudius Glaber!

Spartacus' revenge

One of Spartacus' jobs as a gladiator had been to fight at funeral games. When he won a battle against a Roman general he gave him a great funeral – he made the Roman prisoners fight to the death. It was his way of taking revenge.

Suffering Spartacus

But in the end Spartacus' slave army couldn't beat General Crassus and his huge Roman army – it took ten legions (about 60,000 men) to beat the rebels. Six thousand of Spartacus' rebels were captured and all of them were crucified. Crassus placed the crosses at the sides of the main road into Rome as a lesson.

Ruthless Roman quiz

The Romans could be nasty – and so can *you*! All you have to do is turn off your television and hide the remote control. Then say to your foul family, 'Right! You don't get the telly back unless you get at least five of these foul Roman facts correct!' That's ruthless. Here are the questions…

1 What did King Tarquinius Priscus do to people who committed suicide?
a) eat them
b) crucify them
c) play football with their heads

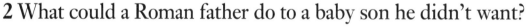

... AND TARQUINIUS GOES AHEAD WITH A HEADED HEAD!

2 What could a Roman father do to a baby son he didn't want?
a) leave it outside the city to die
b) throw it in the river to swim for its life
c) feed it to the family dogs

3 What dangerous game would some Romans try for a bet?
a) boxing with a bear
b) swimming with piranhas
c) running with their shirt on fire

BYE BYE

4 What would toilet cleaners do with the poo they collected?
a) sell it
b) eat it
c) tip it in a bog

5 When a traitor was beheaded in Rome, what happened to his head?

a) it was stuck on a spike

b) it was thrown into the sewers

c) its brains were eaten by the emperor

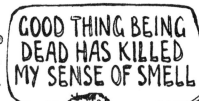

6 What was your punishment if you killed your father?

a) you'd get the sack

b) you'd be eaten by an elephant

c) you'd be strangled by your mother

7 Why did the Romans have trouble burying the traitors Drusus and Nero?

a) because they weren't dead and kept digging their way out of the grave

b) because they were so fat they couldn't find any coffins that were big enough

c) because they'd been chopped into so many small pieces

8 Rome was able to grow to be a great city because of its sewers. How big were they?

a) big enough for a man to crawl through

b) big enough for a 12-year-old boy to walk through without bending

c) big enough for a horse and cart with a load of hay to drive through

9 Romans fought and raced in an 'arena'. The word 'arena' meant 'sand'. Why was there sand in the arena?

a) to soak up all the blood

b) so it was soft for fighters to fall on

c) so fighters could pick up a handful and throw it in an enemy's eyes

THAT REALLY IS SOFT

10 What terrible torture did the Romans sometimes use on Christian women?

a) they tied them to a post and tickled them with giant ostrich feathers

b) they put them in a catapult and flung them high in the air

c) they hung them from a post by their long hair

Answers:

1b) King Tarquinius made poor Romans work on digging out the sewers for the city. It was back-breaking work. Many workers decided to kill themselves rather than get out of bed to go to work. (Even today a lot of people feel the same about work.) The King said, 'These people must not rest peacefully in their graves. Crucify them so the others can see what will happen if they commit suicide. Let them see the crows peck out their eyes and rats tear their flesh!' Nice man.

2 Usually **a)**. A Roman father had the power of life and death over his children. If he decided he couldn't afford to feed a new baby, he would leave it out to be saved by someone else, or die. But many Roman babies were thrown to dogs or drowned, or killed and then put on the city rubbish dump. Most of those babies were probably girls – worth less than Roman boys.

3c) Wearing a flaming tunic was a punishment for criminals. But sometimes Romans would wear one of those tunics and bet they could run, say, 100 metres before tearing it off. (Don't tell your teachers about this or they may decide to try that game at the next school sports day.)

4a) Not everyone was connected to Rome's wonderful sewers. Many houses let their toilet waste drain into a deep pit. But in time the pit filled with poo. Toilet cleaners would shovel it out, load it on carts and take it to sell to farmers. The farmers would spread it on their fields to help their crops grow.

5b) The idea was that you couldn't get into heaven if your head wasn't buried with your body – the gods couldn't have a lot of headless people wandering round, could they? But your body would be thrown in the River Tiber – and the sewers flowed into the same river. So there was just a chance your head and body could get back together! (All right, not much of a chance.)

6a) The 'sack' was a punishment for someone who killed a parent. Emperor Claudius loved to watch this form of execution. Claudius sacked more people than any other emperor. The murderer was sewn into a leather sack and thrown into the river to drown. Often there would be a snake, a monkey, a dog and a cockerel sewn in with the victim so they were clawed and bitten by the terrified animals on the way.

7c) Two brothers, Nero and Drusus, were accused of plotting against their great-uncle, Emperor Tiberius. Nero killed himself, but Drusus was shut in the palace cellars and left to starve to death. The brothers were cut into lots of little pieces. In fact there were so many pieces the palace guards had trouble collecting all the bits to bury them!

8c) In 33 BC the Roman General Agrippa had them cleaned out. Agrippa was also an admiral of the navy. His greatest boat trip was to sail through the sewers to check that they were clean. What a way to check a job. That's what's called 'thorough'. Still, from time to time, the sewers did get blocked and the forum was flooded with sewage. You'd have to hitch up your toga and paddle through poo.

9a) The sand soaked up the blood – sometimes. But after very gory fights or animal massacres there were slaves sent in to scatter fresh sand. Still, the rotting blood must have smelled pretty awful.

10b) In the city of Tyre in Carthage, in the AD 400s, the Christian women were stripped naked and thrown into the air by the Romans. There was no one to catch them.

Empire timeline

In AD 14, Augustus Caesar, the first Roman emperor, dies. The next 400 years will see a mix of good and bad emperors – but mostly bad.

AD **31** Emperor Tiberius had retired to Capri island in AD 26 and left the country to be run by Sejanus – leader of the army in Rome. But Sejanus started bumping off rivals so he could be next emperor. In AD 31 Tiberius had Sejanus (and his two children) strangled.

AD **37** Cruel Tiberius dies. Romans are happy – little do they know the next emperor, Caligula, will be much, much worse! He lasts four years before they murder him.

AD **43** Emperor Claudius arranges to have a little island invaded. It is Britain – and the Romans will stay for 350 years.

AD **64** Claudius dies from eating poisoned mushrooms and nutty Nero takes over. In AD 64, a huge fire destroys much of Rome and Nero is blamed. He says, 'It was those Jews that follow Jesus Christ! Blame *them*!' The Romans do and start hundreds of years of cruel executions of Christians.

AD 79 Mount Vesuvius erupts and buries Pompeii in southern Italy. Plenty of suffocated victims for historians to dig up in later years.

AD 80 The Colosseum is built in Rome – a nice big place to murder criminals and Christians for fun.

AD 117 Emperor Hadrian finds he is fighting on all sides just to keep the Roman Empire together. He builds a great wall across the north of England to keep out the northern Celts – the Scots. (But they still get in.)

AD 161 Emperor Marcus Aurelius thinks the Empire is too big and decides to share it. This is the beginning of two Roman Empires – the East and the West. In time they'll fight each other.

AD 165 The armies in the East return with glory – and a plague. It sweeps through the Empire and kills thousands. The Empire will never quite recover its strength.

AD 200s Barbarians start to swarm on Rome – Franks and Alemanni from the north, Goths in Greece and Persians in the Middle-East – where they even captured Emperor Valerian in AD 260. Valerian was then skinned alive and his skin put on display. And when they aren't

fighting Barbarians, the Romans are fighting each other – no one can decide who should be the emperor.

AD **300s** Emperor Diocletian sorts out the Empire but retires in AD 305. The Empire is split again – with two emperors. Of course, they fight. Constantine eventually takes control of the whole Empire. He is a Christian who ended the killing of Christians in the arena – but not the animal hunts and the gladiator contests.

AD **378** The Visigoths have run away from the horrible Huns – Barbarians living in eastern Europe – but the Romans are not too pleased to see them and try to keep them out, so the Visigoths force their way into the Roman Empire and become invaders.

AD **410** The Visigoths take Rome and then Rome is open to attacks from everyone.

AD **476** The last Roman emperor in the West loses his throne. His name, like that of the first Rome leader, is Romulus. Very neat.

Evil emperors

Augustus Caesar became the first Roman emperor. The trouble was he was a *good* emperor ... so the Romans thought it was a *good* idea to have them. But even when some bad, mad and sad men became emperors, the Romans didn't give up on the idea – they just murdered the man and got a new one!

Here are a few of the foulest...

Horrible Histories Warning: Some of these terrible tales were told by the emperor's enemies. There may be a bit of foul fibbing in some cases. Don't believe everything you read in a history book!

Tiberius (AD 14–37)

Cruel Tiberius retired at the age of 67 and spent the last ten years of his life on the island of Capri – an island with some useful cliffs...

Five foul facts

- Tiberius had his enemies tortured then thrown off the cliffs into the sea, while he watched. Just to make sure they didn't survive there were sailors waiting at the bottom to smash the victims with boat-hooks and oars.
- His sister-in-law, Agrippina, was banished to Pandateria island off the western coast of Italy and beaten so badly that one of her eyes was destroyed. She starved herself to death.
- Her son, Drusus, was arrested and locked in a cell to starve. He even tried to eat the stuffing in his mattress.
- Tiberius fell ill and the next emperor, Caligula, took the imperial ring off the finger of the dying man ... then Tiberius sat up and asked for food! The commander of the

guards went into the room. Instead of food he had a cushion with him to finish off the dying old man.

• Tiberius was hated – even though Rome was peaceful while he ruled. He was remembered in two words…

Caligula (AD 37–41)

Caligula wasn't his real name. He was really called Emperor Gaius. But he was born in an army camp and loved to wear little soldier boots. The name for little boots was 'Caligula' and that became his nickname. But when he grew up he hated being called that and punished anyone who did. Mind you, he didn't like the name Gaius much either!

Five foul facts

• He made mothers and fathers come along to watch their children being executed. That was sweet, wasn't it? If you were executed you'd like your mum there, wouldn't you?

• Caligula had his chief animal-keeper flogged with chains, day after day. At last the man's leaking brains started to smell so Caligula had him killed.

• Caligula often made his feasts more fun by having someone tortured as he ate. At one dinner he brought in a slave who had stolen a strip of silver from a couch; executioners lopped off the man's hands, tied them round his neck and took him for a tour of the tables, with a sign showing what he had done to deserve it.

225

- Caligula had a very hairy body, like a goat. So you'd be executed if you said the word 'goat' while you were with him.

- Caligula shocked Romans because he loved to dress up. He dressed up as Roman gods like Jupiter … that was silly but harmless. The Romans really gasped when they saw Caligula dressed in a jewelled dress as the goddess Venus. He even robbed the grave of Alexander the Great so he could dress in the dead man's armour and pretend to be him.

Did you know…?
A fortune-teller once told Caligula…

When Caligula become emperor he still had to take his revenge on the fortune-teller by riding across the bay without wetting his horse's shoes.

And in AD 39 he did it. How? He had a bridge of boats floated across the Bay of Baiae and joined by planks. He then rode across. It was two miles long. The next day he rode back in a chariot. But Caligula had used just about every boat in Rome. The owners of the boats (and lots of Roman shopkeepers) lost a lot of money because they couldn't trade for a week.

Claudius (AD 41–54)

Emperor Claudius enjoyed games in the arena, watching people torn apart by other people or by animals. But there was one thing he *stopped*. What?

a) a gladiator chopping the head off a swan because it was such a beautiful bird

b) hunters chasing a bull on horseback because the horses were getting hurt

c) a lion eating a human being because he thought it was disgusting

Answer: **c)** Most wild animals in the arena tore humans to death but they did not eat them. (It's a fact that wild animals rarely eat humans.) But one lion had been specially trained to eat human flesh after it had killed its victim. The crowd loved it. Claudius didn't – what a kind man! So Claudius had the lion killed ... well, not *all that kind*, then.

Nero (AD 54–68)

There is no doubt that Emperor Nero was mad. For a start, he told people he was a god and anyone who refused to call him a god ended up in the sewers.

Nero also used to enjoy roaming the streets of Rome, beating up men as they went home for dinner. If they tried to fight back he stabbed them and their bodies ended up in the sewers.

Five foul facts

- Nero loved singing and performing – but no one was allowed to leave the theatre, even though Nero went on for hours and hours. Historian Suetonius said…

But Suetonius didn't like Nero and that may just be a joke and a bit of a fib.

- Among Nero's most disgusting hobbies was to keep a 'glutton' – a monstrous Egyptian slave who ate everything

228

and anything he was fed. It was said that Nero really enjoyed watching his glutton kill a human and eat him.

- Nero loved his wife, Poppaea, dearly – he had his first wife murdered so he could marry Poppaea. But his love didn't stop him kicking her to death when they had a row.
- Nero murdered his step-brother, two wives and his mother. But he didn't murder his teacher, Seneca. Instead he just told him…

Seneca cut his own wrists. You wouldn't treat your old teacher like that, would you? (Better not answer that!)
- When the army came to throw Nero off his throne it was his turn to commit suicide. But he made a mess of stabbing himself in the neck and a servant had to finish him off.

Did you know…?
Nero was a winner at the AD 67 Olympics – even though he lost! He rode in the ten-horse chariot race … and fell off. But they gave him the prize because: **a)** they said, 'He would have won if he *hadn't* fallen off' and **b)** they were so scared of him they didn't dare let him lose!

Vitellius (AD 69)

This emperor was famous for eating like a pig. He had four feasts a day and often tickled the back of his throat with a feather till he vomited – then he had room for more food. His favourite snacks were livers of pike fish, brains of pheasants and tongues of flamingos.

Even though he loved food, his enemies said Vitellius starved his own mother to death.

Domitian (AD 81–96)

Domitian took over when his brother, Emperor Titus, died, and people soon learned to hate and fear him…

Five foul facts

- Emperor Domitian was always afraid that someone would stab him in the back. So he had his palace walls built of polished white marble so they shone like mirrors. That way, he could see who was behind him!
- Domitian was touchy about his bald head. When painters painted his picture they showed him with long, flowing hair.
- One of his habits was catching flies, stabbing them with the point of a pen and tearing their wings off.
- He was just as cruel to humans. He hated Jews and had them hunted down and executed.

- The priestesses of the goddess Vesta were not supposed to have boyfriends but he suspected them of having lovers and had four women executed – the chief priestess was buried alive and the boyfriends beaten to death with rods.

Commodus (AD 180–192)

Emperor Commodus fancied himself as a gladiator and trained with them. But he only fought with blunt weapons against feeble opponents.

Five foul facts
- Criminals were sometimes given stones to throw to defend themselves in the arena. That was too risky for Commodus. The Roman writer Dio Cassius said…

He once got together all the men in the city who had lost their feet from disease or accident. He tied their knees together and gave them sponges to throw instead of stones. He killed them with blows from a club, pretending they were giants.

- Dio had a problem. He had to stop himself laughing when he watched Commodus strut around the arena pretending to be a hero. Dio chewed bitter laurel leaves to keep the smile off his face as Commodus pranced about, proudly holding up the head of his victim … an ostrich. If Dio had laughed then Commodus would probably have had him executed.

- Fighting against Commodus wasn't a laugh for the gladiators, of course, especially the ones he used for practice. One gladiator fought against Commodus with wooden swords. The gladiator decided to make Commodus look good and he fell to the ground. So Commodus drew a *real* knife and stabbed the man to death. Even when he wasn't trying to kill his opponents he could somehow do it. Dio explained…

> *When he was training Commodus managed to kill a man now and then. And he enjoyed making close swings at others as if trying to shave off a bit of their hair. But instead he often sliced off the noses of some, the ears of others and different parts of still others.*

SNICK! YOW

LOP! OUCH

- In the arena, Commodus never shed human blood – he killed animals but only fought humans with blunted weapons. Shedding human blood would be a disgraceful thing for an emperor to do!
- Romans went along to the games to watch other people die horribly. But when Commodus was in charge the visitors sometimes found themselves dragged into the arena to be victims. Imagine going to a boxing match and being told…

WE'VE DECIDED TO GIVE YOU A GO!

Valentinian I (364–375)

Emperor Valentinian had a cage near his bedroom where he kept man-killing bears. For fun, Valentinian had victims thrown into the cage where the bears tore them apart. (At least, when I say 'for fun', I mean it was fun for Val, but probably not for the victims.) Kind-hearted Valentinian set his pet bears free after they had torn dozens of people apart.

Ending emperors

Being emperor could be a dangerous job. Lots of people wanted your throne – and lots were ready to kill you to get it. Of course, you had your own bodyguard – the Praetorian guard, who were the only soldiers living in the city of Rome. The trouble was that often the Praetorian guard *themselves* wanted to get rid of you.

Who could an emperor trust? Answer – no one! Lots of emperors met grisly and gruesome deaths…

Wicked wives

Some empresses were as bad as emperors, taking part in plots to murder their husbands, their enemies and even their own children. The first empress was suspected of killing her husband, Emperor Augustus, to make sure her own son became the next emperor. Writer Tacitus said she'd worked out a way to harm hubby – and get away with it…

233

Livia lived on. She died at the age of 86. Her son, Emperor Tiberius, refused to go to her funeral.

Getting it down the throat

Emperor Claudius became ill with diarrhoea … well, it's not surprising really. His wife had fed him poisoned mushrooms! She was afraid he would recover, though, so she came up with a new plot. The doctor went to Claudius and said, 'It would help if you were sick.' He then tickled the back of the Emperor's throat with a feather. But the feather had been dipped in a deadly poison. That finished him off.

234

Flying eye

Emperor Domitian's wife was part of the plot to kill him. An ex-slave was sent to stab him – but the first cut didn't kill the Emperor and he fought back, trying to gouge out the attacker's eyes. In the end the other plotters had to rush into the room and hack him enough times to finish him off. Very messy – and his bloody corpse was probably covered in flies who wanted to party.

Drained to death

Emperor Elagabalus was not a nice man. He said to the Praetorian guard:

But the soldiers, who rather liked Alexander, said:

He turned to the soldiers' officers and ordered:

But the officers said:

Elagabalus knew he had a problem ... his own soldiers wanted him dead – and he was surrounded by them. So he hid himself in a trunk and arranged to have himself carried out secretly. But he was discovered and ran for shelter – into a toilet!

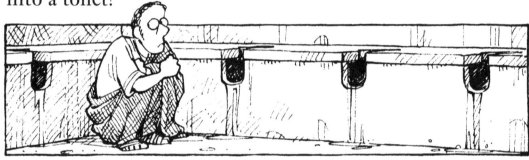

A Roman described what happened...

Next the soldiers fell on Elagabalus and killed him in the toilet where he was hiding. Then his body was dragged through the streets and round the arena. The soldiers insulted the corpse again by stuffing it into a sewer. But the sewer was too small to take the body. They took it out and threw it from the Aemilian Bridge into the Tiber.

The main sewer of Rome was big enough to take some bodies, though, and quite a few victims ended up down there among the poo.

236

Promise for the patient

Many Romans made wild promises when Emperor Caligula fell ill. They gathered outside his palace and carried banners.

The trouble is, Caligula got better … and made the men keep their promises! The writer Suetonius wrote…

A man had offered his life but didn't kill himself. Caligula handed the man over to his slaves. They were ordered to carry him through the streets, decorated with holy tree branches and finally throw him into the river.

Did you know…?

Emperor Caligula was killed in a narrow passageway. So narrow, the guards who planned to assassinate him had to queue up to stick a sword in him. Some of them happily stabbed Caligula in his naughty bits.

Pleb pun

Miserable, grouchy Emperor Tiberius hardly ever gave the people games in the arena and they learned to hate him. So, when he died, they had a party in the streets of Rome. They wanted his body dragged off and thrown in the River Tiber so they chanted a little Latin joke, over and over…

You don't need me to tell you what that means. You do? Oh, all right. 'Tiberius to the Tiber'. It's a bit like Americans chanting 'Mrs Hippy in the Mississippi' or Germans singing 'Rhinos in the Rhine' or Egyptians crying 'Neil in the Nile!' or … Chinese calling 'Nancy in the Yangtse' or … oh, you can make up your own.

Not a great joke, but it's hard to be funny at funerals. Anyway, the plebs didn't get what they wanted. The soldiers burned Tiberius to ashes. And it's not easy dragging a pile of ashes with a hook.

Getting it in the neck

Commodus liked to act as a gladiator, but gladiators were often common criminals and the Romans hated seeing their emperor making a fool of himself.

Commodus set off to a great ceremony where he would be made a consul and wear gladiator's armour. That was too much for the Romans – a bit like a king going to be crowned dressed as a tramp. So his enemies fed him poison the night before the event – but Commodus threw up. In the end an athlete, Narcissus, was sent to finish off the Emperor by strangling him – just as though he were the common criminal he pretended to be.

238

He was buried at night and the government (the Roman senate) demanded that…

HE SHOULD BE DUG UP AND DRAGGED AROUND THE CITY LIKE A CRIMINAL. THAT'S WHAT HE DID TO OTHERS – LET'S DO IT TO HIM!

They didn't. Commodus was left to rest in peace – and four years later Emperor Septimius Severus made him a god.

A few foul facts

Yes, you too can learn these facts and repeat them at the tea table. Shock your aunties and disgust your grannies. (That's what they were invented for, isn't it?) Invite them round to tea and make sure you've got plenty of food on the table.

DELIGHTFUL, CHILDREN. HOW NICE!

Then tell them the following...

1 Did you know that Julius Caesar entertained the Romans with mock battles? In one he had two armies with 500 foot-soldiers, 20 elephants and 30 horsemen. So many people crowded in to see these games that a lot of spectators were crushed to death. (Squeeze a chocolate éclair till the cream gushes out as you say 'crushed' – and use red food-colouring to make the cream look like blood if you like.)

2 Did you know that in AD 80 Titus had games lasting 100 days? Nine thousand animals were killed in the fighting. Some of the animals were wild and some were tame pets! (As you say 'tame pets' pick up granny's cat and stroke it with an evil look in your eye.)

240

3 Did you know that in 355 BC the Romans took 358 captives from posh Tarquinian families? They took them to the marketplace, where first they flogged them then they cut off their heads. (A jelly baby would be good to use to show this horror. But don't use a sharp knife and cut yourself. Just tear the head off.)

4 Did you know that if a Roman owed a lot of people money they could all take a slice of him with a knife in payment? (Cut into a tomato and show how little slices can be hacked off – very messily.)

5 Did you know that the Romans had gladiator fights at their feasts? Nicolaus of Damascus said…

When they were full with food and drink they called in the gladiators. No sooner did one have his throat cut than the masters clapped with delight.

(Follow this with a squirt of tomato ketchup. Hold the ketchup bottle close to your neck.)

6 Did you know that a Roman traitor would be thrown off a high cliff – the Tarpeian Rock? (Spread a good dollop of strawberry jam on a bun. That's what the victim would look like at the bottom.)

7 Did you know the Romans had wonderful sewers that flowed into the River Tiber? The fish fed on the sewage – and the Romans then ate those fish. So, really, they ended up eating their own poo! (Lick your lips as you spear a sardine with your fork and munch it.)

8 Did you know, a Roman emperor called Vitellius invented a pie made from the tongues of flamingos and the brains of peacocks? (Take a scoop of ice-cream as you say 'peacock brains' and swallow it while saying, 'Mmmm! Gorgeous.')

9 Did you know that Emperor Elagabalus was fond of eating camel heels? (Tricky one, this. You may have to pop to the supermarket and ask for a pack of deep-fried camel heels. Serve them with jelly and say, 'Have a dish of jellied heels!')

10 Did you know, the first Romans didn't use money – they used salt! (Take the salt cellar and pour it over granny's treacle pudding, saying, 'Here's that five quid I owe you!')

Marvellous medicine

Roman medicine was a mixture of common sense and daftness. Many doctors were Greek slaves who had been set free – because the groovy Greeks knew more than the Romans about medicine. Other men became doctors because they were useless at everything else they tried – a bit like traffic wardens today. And, like traffic wardens today, Roman doctors often hung around on street corners. They would try to attract patients…

The doctors followed drunks home from the taverns, looking for business…

It's said that the doctors even told rude jokes to the drunks to try to get them to part with their money…

Here are ten foul facts:

1 If you suffered from epilepsy then there was a gruesome cure…

GIVE HER A DRINK OF THE WARM BLOOD FROM A DEAD GLADIATOR. THE FRESHER THE BETTER

I'LL JUST POP DOWN TO THE ARENA THEN

2 In early Rome medicine was made and dished out by the head of the family, i.e. dad.

3 The first Greek doctor in Rome was a man called Arcagathus, in 219 BC. He was very popular at first. But he used to let a lot of blood out of patients as a 'cure' and that often killed them. He became known as 'The Executioner'.

4 The Roman surgeons had some simple painkillers for doing operations. In one operation they would drill into a patient's skull – but they did NOT use the painkiller for that!

NO PAIN, NO GAIN!

5 Romans enjoyed their public baths, but the sick and the well bathed together so they helped spread disease! Plus from time to time some plague would sweep through one of their towns – but the Romans often blamed poisoners, instead! (There *were* people in Rome who were paid to go around poisoning people. Men like Canidia, Martina and Locusta would take your money and bump off your enemy. Locusta took Emperor Nero's money and killed his brother, Britannicus.)

6 Cato was a Roman magistrate. He wrote down some useful cures that you may like to try on someone you don't like:

244

7 The Roman Diodorus had a twisted spine and hated his hunched back. Doctor Socles promised to set the back straight. (Don't try this at home!) The doctor lay the patient on the floor and took three stones (each over a metre square), then he placed the stones on Diodorus' back. What happened next? The good news: Diodorus' back was straight as a ruler! The bad news: he was crushed to death.

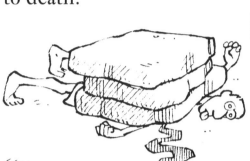

8 Emperor Caligula had a favourite gladiator called Columbus. But Columbus let him down and was defeated in the arena. Caligula said…

But the ointment was poisoned. Columbus did not live – if he had he may have sailed off and discovered America. But that was left to another bloke from Italy called … er … er … I've forgotten.

9 Rome's most famous doctor was the Greek, Galen. But some of his advice to doctors looks a bit odd today. Galen said…

10 Galen was not allowed to cut up corpses. So he found out how the human body worked by cutting up monkeys (which are a lot like humans) and cattle (which aren't). That must have led to some mistakes…

Awful for animals

Want some fun in ancient Rome? Then kill an animal – or use an animal to kill a human. The Romans had animal-hunting games – 'venationes' they called them – in their arenas. Where did they get that idea from? Pinched it, of course.

Around 600 BC, an Etruscan drew a savage sketch. A blindfolded man, armed with a club, is being attacked by a dog. A masked man with a whip watches.

So what is going on in that sketch? It *may* just be an early example of the 'games' people liked to watch. Some historians say this is what the sketch means…

- The victim is blindfolded and thrown in a ring with a starving, mad dog.
- He can defend himself with the club – and even kill the dog – except he can't see what he is hitting. It's a bit like blind-man's buff with teeth.

- The man with the whip is there to make sure the victim doesn't run away.
- The dog dies or the man dies – either way the crowd has excitement and blood.

This may be an Etruscan idea the Romans borrowed. Other historians think the animal-hunting idea came from Persia. Persian King Ashburnipal used to massacre wild animals to show what a brave man he was. Sometimes he chased them in his chariot – but sometimes they were brought to him in cages. They were set free and the King then killed them while his people watched. Did this lead to this awful ancient joke?

FOOLISH SLAVE! WHERE IS THE GLORY IN KILLING A BUDGIE?

I GOT IT BECAUSE IT WAS GOING CHEAP!

Etruscan idea? Persian idea? Who cares? The result was still a lot of dead animals. And hunting, sacrificing and torturing animals certainly gave the Romans a lot of their fun. In Rome it could be really awful for animals...

Fiery for foxes

At harvest time it was a custom to catch a fox, wrap it in straw and set the straw alight. The flaming fox would then be left to run off and die in terror and agony. The Romans probably believed this would teach all vermin a lesson – 'Stay away from our crops or else this may happen to you!'

The custom may have come from a tale of a farm boy from Carseoli who punished a fox this way when he caught it stealing chickens. But the burning fox ran into a cornfield, set fire to the crop and destroyed it.

Evil for elephants

Elephants were great in battle. Send elephants charging at the enemy and they'll run for their lives. They were a bit like tanks – 2,000 years before tanks were invented and 2,000 years before this joke was...

The great general from Carthage, Hannibal, used elephants to scare the Romans. He also had a gladiator idea – he made prisoners fight one another and the winner would go free. This was to teach the soldiers of Carthage that death in a fight is better than death as a prisoner. Then one day he had a really bright idea...

Rotten for rhinos

Most animals fought against gladiators or against other animals in the arena. Even if they won they were then killed by hunters or dogs. But some animals became favourites of the crowd. They fought bravely and the crowd decided they should live. One rhinoceros fought so well the crowd loved it. What did they do to this two-tonne terror?

a) They set it free. (It could cause a lot of laughs if it was set free in the marketplace!)

b) They ate it. (You get a lot of rhino-burgers out of one rhino.)

c) They sent it to fight again. (If he keeps winning he could be heavyweight champion of the world!)

Answer: **c)** The same rhino fought time and again in the arena for emperors Titus and Domitian.

Brutal for bears

Emperor Commodus saw himself as a brave fighter and a daring hunter. He liked to go to the arena and kill animals. In fact, he was a cowardy custard and never came near the animals in case he got hurt. At one show he had 100 bears put in the arena and then climbed on to a platform where the bears couldn't reach him. Then he threw spears or fired arrows till all the bears were dead.

You may think that is a disgusting and cruel thing to do – don't worry, most of the Romans at that time would have agreed with you. Commodus was murdered – and his sister may have been part of the plot.

Beastly for bears

A Roman leader in Greece gathered a large number of bears for an arena hunt. But the weather was so hot the bears died and were dumped in the streets. The poor people of the town came along with knives, carved up the animals, cooked them and ate them. Bears were supposed to attack people in the arena – but this time people ate the bears!

A Roman woman, the wife of Habinnas, ate bear flesh – and almost threw up. Habinnas himself said it was tasty – a bit like wild boar.

Gory goring

Wild boars were often put into the arena to gore victims with their sharp tusks. A really nasty trick was to tie a victim to the belly of a boar and let the maddened beast roll and kick and bite at the human. An animal keeper was tying a Christian to a boar like this when the boar used its tusks to gore the keeper.

Dreadful for dogs

In the reign of Emperor Tiberius a Roman called Sabinus was sentenced to death – along with all his slaves – for treason. But there was one loyal friend who wasn't put to death and stayed with him till the very end. His dog. Here's how the story goes…

There were a lot of witnesses, so this incredible tale of a faithful friend could well be true.

Lousy for lions

Emperor Caligula showed off his courage by entering the arena with a lion. Caligula carried a club – which was more than the poor lion had because it would probably have had its teeth and claws ripped out so it was no danger to the Emperor.

Of course it wasn't all lousy for lions. There is a famous story about a Christian called Androcles, a runaway African slave, who took a thorn from a lion's paw in the wild. Androcles was caught and sentenced to death in the arena; but he met the same lion in the arena and the lion refused to eat him. (Believe that if you like.) The Roman writer Apion said...

Androcles was set free and presented with the lion. Afterwards we used to see Androcles with the lion on a thin lead, going round the taverns of Rome. Androcles was given money, the lion was sprinkled with flowers and everyone loved to see them.

IF I SAID I WASN'T HAPPY I'D BE LION

What sort of flowers would you throw at the animal? *Dandelions*, of course.

The lion's tale

This is supposed to be a true story...

> ʘOnce upon a time there was a ferocious lion that hated men. He was fastened in a cage and longed to be free.
>
> From time to time men with whips came for him and chased him into a sandy arena. Thousands of human eyes watched him as he prowled and paced around the circle, looking for something to eat.
>
> Then he would hear the clank of a gate and the thousands of humans would raise their voices in a scream and he knew that meant it was dinner-time. He knew that some scrawny, scraggy human had been thrown into the arena and he would tear that victim apart.

Sometimes the victim knelt and prayed, sometimes they wept, sometimes they screamed and tried to run. But the end was always the same.

There was only one human the lion liked. His keeper. Every day the keeper brought him food and water and talked to him and stroked  him. In the stinking, gloomy, miserable cage it was the lion's only happiness.

Then one day the keeper didn't come. The lion lay on the damp, dark floor and sulked until men came with whips and drove him out into the scorching sun of the arena. On that day a bear and a leopard were there. (The Romans sometimes put in a few animals to kill the human and then watched them fight over the flesh.) The lion padded round and watched the bear and the leopard, and they watched him.

Then he heard the clank. The gate opened and the victim stumbled in. The gate closed behind him.

The lion was the first to leap. With huge bounds and gaping jaws he hurled himself at the man. Then a curious scent met his nostrils and he skidded over the sand as he tried to stop his final leap. It was the scent of his friendly keeper.

'Hello, boy,' the keeper said and the man's eyes were streaming with tears. 'My turn to be eaten, my friend!'

The lion growled.

'Go on. Get it over with. Make it quick!'

The screaming humans had gone curiously quiet. Even the emperor leaned forward from his seat and watched as the keeper stretched out a hand and rubbed the lion's mane. The lion turned his head and licked the man's arm.

Suddenly there was a savage roar and the man fell backwards. The lion saw the leopard leaping at the helpless victim. He threw himself between the leopard and the man. The furious leopard, starving and wild, lashed out with a powerful clawed paw but he was no match for the lion. The lion tore at the leopard and then had to turn suddenly as the bear scented the blood and lumbered towards them. The bear was powerful and his massive claws scarred the lion deeply, but the golden cat hung on till the big brown beast was dead.

The lion turned back to the keeper who was looking on in wonder. The emperor turned to the crowd and cried to them, 'What should I do with him?'

And the crowd roared back, 'Let him live!'

And so the keeper led the lion back out of the gate and his streaming tears were warm on the lion's scarred old nose.

THE END

Dreadful dinners

The wild beasts that ate people in arenas were expensive to train because they had to be fed with large amounts of fresh meat. They were trained by being fed on slaves. But there was always a danger the slave would fight back – and the Romans didn't want their precious beasts hurt by the slaves. So what did they do?

a) The slaves were tied up so they couldn't struggle.

b) The slaves were killed and chopped into pieces before they were fed to the animals.

c) The slaves had their teeth pulled out and their arms broken before being fed to the wild animals.

Answer: **a)** was not good enough because the slave could still bite the animal; **b)** was no use because the animals had to get used to chasing and killing live humans; **c)** was incredibly cruel – but that's what they did.

Emperor Caligula fed criminals to the animals – because it was cheaper than buying meat. He just lined them up, glanced at the prisoners, and gave the order: 'Kill every man between that bald head and the other one over there!' He also ordered that their tongues be cut out so their cries didn't disturb his peace and quiet.

258

Painful plays

Most people enjoy a good play – on television or at the theatre. The Romans didn't have televisions but they did enjoy the theatre. How did it start? I'm glad you asked me that...

The Romans showed their gods how much they loved them by having chariot races in their honour at their 'circus'. The people loved them and they were sure the gods loved them. But in 360 BC a terrible plague hit the city of Rome.

The Romans had more races – but the plague didn't go away. So they asked their Etruscan neighbours for help. The Etruscans sent dancers to perform in the circus. They became really popular with the Romans (and with the gods too, the Romans hoped).

MAYBE THEY SHOULD HAVE STOPPED THE RACES BEFORE THE DANCERS CAME ON

Around 200 BC, a man called Livius Andronicus added a story to the dancing – so it became a sort of mimed play. He pinched stories from the Greeks and soon the Romans had plays to watch.

In time the Romans wrote their own plays and began to mix drama with dreadful doings...

Theatre to make you throw up

You've watched murder stories, haven't you? But you know the blood is fake and the actors don't really get hurt at all. The Romans had a better idea. They would act out violent stories and, at the last minute, put a criminal on stage and *really* hurt him. It was real blood and real death the Romans wanted to watch.

- In some plays the criminal was dressed in golden clothes and had to dance happily for the audience. Then suddenly the clothes would be set on fire and he'd be burned to death. This sort of execution was called 'crematio'.
- A Christian writer complained that the Romans showed their gods on stage, dancing over the real blood and bodies of criminals. The god Attis was acted by a criminal, and the Roman audience watched as he had his naughty bits cut off – for real. The writer said that…

A criminal playing the god Hercules was burned alive.

I ALWAYS WANTED MY FLAME-UP IN TIGHTS

- The actors in Roman plays were often slaves, who might expect a beating if the audience didn't like them.
- Hardly any Roman playwrights bothered to invent their own stories. They just pinched them from Greek plays and wrote them in Latin.
- The Roman writer Terence complained that one of his plays was deserted by the spectators. They got up and walked out in the middle of it. Why?

   a) The audience was disgusted because there was too much violence – they heard there was some peaceful music being played in the forum and left.

   b) The audience was disgusted because there was not enough violence – they heard there was a gladiator fight to the death in another arena and left.

   c) An actor fell off the stage and broke a leg – the audience couldn't wait for a replacement to arrive so they left.

Answer: **b)** Terence complained that this happened *twice* during his plays. Audiences rushed out to watch a tight-rope walker or a boxing match. If they grew bored with the plays they yelled out...

Maybe Terence should have written better plays, eh? Plays like this one...

Sickening scene

The plays themselves could be disgusting. In a scene from a story by Lucius Apuleius a gang of men talk about how they will punish a girl who's annoyed them. You might like to act this out in your next drama lesson – but make sure there is a sick bucket handy for the teacher...

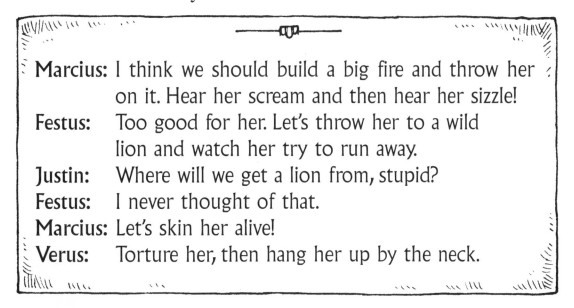

Marcius: I think we should build a big fire and throw her on it. Hear her scream and then hear her sizzle!

Festus: Too good for her. Let's throw her to a wild lion and watch her try to run away.

Justin: Where will we get a lion from, stupid?

Festus: I never thought of that.

Marcius: Let's skin her alive!

Verus: Torture her, then hang her up by the neck.

Ferox:	No! Listen to me. All these are too quick. We want her to suffer.
Justin:	So what would you do?
Ferox:	There's an old donkey in our field and it kicks and bites and won't work.
Festus:	A bit like you, Justin!
Ferox:	Let's kill the donkey and take out its guts.
Verus:	I thought we were going to kill the girl!
Ferox:	I'm coming to that. We tie her up and put her in the donkey's belly. Then we sew it up with just her head sticking out.
Marcius:	That's good, Ferox. Then we put the dead donkey on a high rock in the midday sun till she roasts.
Justin:	When the wild animals start to tear the donkey apart...
Verus:	...they'll start to tear her apart!
Ferox:	And when she's almost dead we'll hang her from the gallows and let the dogs and vultures tear her guts out.
Festus:	Where do we start?
Ferox:	Justin and Marcius, catch the girl – Verus and I will kill the donkey!
	(The men cackle horribly and leave the stage)

Nasty story. But the really horrible thing is the writer probably got the idea from some truly terrible punishments he'd seen in Rome. There are stories about two soldiers being sewn into the bellies of two oxen – while the animals were still alive! The soldiers' heads were left out so they

262

could talk to one another and each see the other suffer. But some historians think that story may not be true.

You could perform this little play for your class during school assembly. But don't forget to tell them...

Cruel for criminals

The Romans didn't mess about when they caught criminals. Punishments were painful. Very painful. And many of them were made into shows for the public to watch.

Copy-cat crosses

The Romans liked crucifying people – nailing them to a cross and letting them die slowly. But they probably didn't invent crucifixion. The Persians had crucifixion first and the Romans thought, 'Oh, what a great idea! Look at how those victims are suffering!'

The Emperor Constantine ruled from AD 307–337. He banned crucifixion…

A wooden fork was built – the shape of a 'Y' – and the criminal's neck was placed in the fork. He was left to dangle there and choke to death.

Cruel Constantine

In the reign of Emperor Constantine (one of the 'kindest' emperors) there were over 60 crimes that could get you executed. He also invented a new type of execution ... death by lead. Here's how he did it. *Don't try this at home.*

As you know, lead is poisonous! So watch out when you chew those pencils!

Terrible Tiberius

Emperor Tiberius was definitely *not* a kindly emperor. A Roman nobleman had some coins in his pocket, which had the head of Tiberius stamped on them, of course. When the consul went to the toilet with the coins in his pocket Tiberius was furious! Having a pee in front of his face on the coins? How dare he? Tiberius had the man executed.

There is another story of a man who went for a pee at a banquet wearing a ring with the face of Tiberius on it. He might have been executed but a slave saved his life by stopping him from peeing!

Tiberius also had a man called Sextius Paconianus strangled in prison for making fun of him. But Sextius wasn't the only one who made fun of Tiberius. The sort of insulting things written about him were verses like:

He is not thirsty for good wine.
As he was thirsty then,
He warms him up a tastier cup –
The blood of murdered men.

Another poet wrote…

You monster! I'll be surprised, I will,
If even your mother loves you still.

Not surprisingly, perhaps, Tiberius had a poet called Aelius Saturninus thrown off the Tarpeian Rock for an insulting poem he'd written…

I SAID THAT TIBERIUS IS FAT,
I DIDN'T SEE MUCH WRONG IN THAT.
UNLESS I CAN FLY,
I'M SOON GOING TO DIE,
WHEN MY HEAD HITS THE GROUND AND GOES...

SPLOT!

Did you know...?

Tiberius made it a crime to change your clothes in front of a statue of the first Roman emperor, Augustus Caesar. (Mind you, these reports were all written by someone who didn't like Tiberius so they may not be completely true.)

Horrible historians!

In Rome it could be dangerous writing history books! Hermogenes of Tarsus was executed by Emperor Domitian for what he put in his history book. But the scribes who copied out the book for Hermogenes were also executed. They were crucified.

History writers today can get nasty letters, but those scribes got just *one* letter, a big 'X', and they were nailed to it.

Cutting comments

Emperor Caligula had people executed if they didn't enjoy the gladiator shows he put on for them. At one games Caligula brought a knight before him and accused him of picking faults with the show...

Pelted and pongy

Criminals were often executed quietly by being strangled in jail. But the most-hated criminals were executed in public so the Roman people could join in.

Emperor Vitellius faced a rebellion in AD 69 and lost. The rebels were coming to get him so he tried to disguise himself in rags and hoped his enemies wouldn't find him. But they did. The writer Suetonius described what happened next...

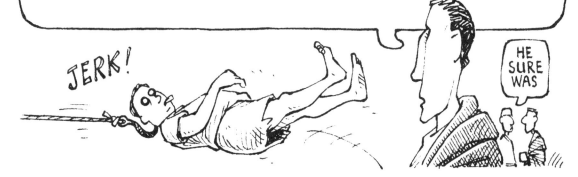

> *The soldiers tied his arms behind his back, put a noose around his neck and dragged him in his torn clothes to the forum. All along the way the crowds greeted him with cruel shouts. His head was held back by the hair as they did with common criminals. They pelted him with dogs' droppings. At the forum he was tortured for a long time then killed. His body was dragged off with a hook and thrown into the River Tiber.*

JERK!

HE SURE WAS

The Romans used hooks on hated criminals because they believed they were 'unclean' – no one wanted to touch their dead body.

Punish that person ... properly

Can you match the right Roman punishment to the right Roman crime? It would be criminal if you got too many wrong. So, anyone who gets less than four out of six can punish themselves by writing out 100 times: 'I am not verrey brite.'

Answers:

1f) Yes, throttled for thieving a few field things. (Try saying that fast with a mouth full of stolen cornflakes.)

2d) Of course, if you got away with the lies – and the man in court was executed – you would get all his money! Was it worth the risk? What would you do?

3a) That's right, one Roman who murdered his wife got away with it because, he said, she drank wine. Which reminds me of the ancient Roman joke…

4e) Yes, you'd be burned alive – after being whipped. This is a good example of Romans 'making the punishment fit the crime'. So, a pupil who flicks paper at teacher should be made to eat a book! (Without tomato ketchup.)

5c) Of course, you could escape the clubbing if the name you called someone was true!

6b) A priestess wasn't supposed to have babies but no one was allowed to kill one or the gods would be angry. So she was just fastened in a room (or buried alive) and left to starve or suffocate to death.

Dear oh deer

Romans often tried to make a punishment fit a crime. If you were a poacher who stole someone else's deer you may be sewn into the skin of the deer then set free. After a while hunting dogs would be sent after you. They would think you were a deer (because dogs are a bit stupid like that) and they would tear you to pieces.

Did you know…?
People who were guilty of smaller crimes – maybe pinching food – could be sent to work in mines. But mine work was so hard and dangerous, they died anyway.

Lion in wait for Christians

Christians lived in Rome quite quietly until AD 62. They were a bit odd, the Romans thought, but harmless. Then Rome caught fire and a huge area was burned down. Emperor Nero said…

The Roman people heard about Nero's plan and put two and two together.

So an angry mob marched on Nero and he was in trouble. B-I-G trouble. Nero had to come up with a good story, fast, and he did...

The Romans decided to avenge themselves by killing Christians – and Nero helped a lot. He had the Christians rounded up, tied to poles in his gardens and covered in tar. When it grew dark he held a party in his gardens and, to light up the scene he had the tar-covered Christians set alight.

From then on the Christians suffered another 250 years of torture and death as emperor after emperor sent them to the arena to be torn apart by animals. There were many Christians who died bravely and their stories make grim and gripping reading...

Martyr meat

Thousands of Christians were torn apart in front of cheering Romans. But not all Christians were terrified at the thought. Some actually *wanted* to die because they thought it would be a quick and sure way to get to heaven.

One Christian called Ignatius of Antioch wrote...

> I am writing to all the churches, to say that I will be dying willingly for God's sake, if you do not stop it. Let me be eaten by the beasts. In fact, encourage the wild beasts so their stomachs may become my tomb. Let them eat all of my body, so no one has the trouble of burying me. I long for the beasts that are waiting for me. Or let them kill me with fire, and the cross, and struggles with wild beasts, cutting and tearing me apart, mangling of bones, crushing of my whole body, cruel tortures of the Devil; just so long as I may reach Jesus in heaven.

Brave man.

Pain for Perpetua

Vibia Perpetua lived – and died – in Carthage, North Africa. By March AD 203 she was married with a new-born baby. The region was ruled by the Romans and Vibia Perpetua was guilty of a terrible Roman crime – she was a Christian. Of course, that meant she would be thrown to the wild animals in the arena as many Christians were. All she had to do to avoid this was make a sacrifice to the Roman gods. She didn't have to slit the throat of a goat or chop a chicken. She just had to burn some scented wood – incense – and say, 'God save the Emperor.'

Perpetua refused. She went to prison with her slave, Felicitas, and three other Christian men, Saturus, Saturninus and Revocatus. She had a few weeks to write down her story in a diary...

When I was arrested, my father was angry with me but I stood firm. 'I am a Christian' I said. My father was so angered by the word 'Christian' that he moved towards me as though he would pluck my eyes out. But he left it at that and went away.

We were lodged in the prison; and I was terrified, as I had never before been in such a dark hole. What a difficult time it was! With the crowd the heat was stifling; then there was the extortion of the soldiers; and to crown all, I was tortured with worry for my baby there.

Then I got permission for my baby to stay with me in prison. At once my prison had suddenly become a palace, so that I wanted to be there rather than anywhere else.

The Christians were taken for trial in front of the Roman governor, Hilarianus. Perpetua wrote…

Hilarianus said to me: 'Have pity on your father's grey head; have pity on your infant son. Offer the sacrifice for the

274

> welfare of the Emperors.'
> 'I will not', I retorted.
> 'Are you a Christian?' said Hilarianus.
> And I said: 'Yes I am.'
> When my father persisted in trying to
> dissuade me, Hilarianus ordered him to be
> thrown to the ground and beaten with a
> rod. I felt sorry for father, just as if I
> myself had been beaten. I felt sorry for
> his pathetic old age.

Perpetua and the three other Christian men were sentenced to die on the Emperor's birthday, 7 March. They returned to prison to wait. Meanwhile Perpetua's slave-girl, Felicitas, gave birth to a baby.

In prison Perpetua had a dream of a peaceful heaven and a hard battle against the Devil to get there.

> Then I saw an immense garden, and in it
> a grey-haired man sat in shepherd's garb;
> tall he was, and milking sheep. And
> standing around him were many thousands
> of people clad in white garments. He
> raised his head, looked at me, and said:
> 'I am glad you have come, my child.'

Perpetua was now looking forward to death. Another Christian took up their story on the day of the executions…

THEY MARCHED FROM THE PRISON TO THE ARENA JOYFULLY AS THOUGH THEY WERE GOING TO HEAVEN, WITH CALM FACES, TREMBLING WITH JOY RATHER THAN FEAR. PERPETUA WENT ALONG WITH SHINING FACE AND CALM STEP.

THEY WERE THEN LED UP TO THE GATES AND THE MEN WERE FORCED TO PUT ON THE ROBES OF THE PRIESTS OF SATURN. THE WOMEN WERE FORCED TO DRESS AS THE PRIESTESSES OF CERES. BUT THE NOBLE PERPETUA STRUGGLED TO THE END.

THE GOVERNOR GRANTED HER REQUEST. THEY WERE TO BE BROUGHT INTO THE ARENA JUST AS THEY WERE. PERPETUA THEN BEGAN TO SING A PSALM. AT THIS THE CROWDS BECAME FURIOUS AND CRIED THAT THE CHRISTIANS SHOULD BE WHIPPED. AND THE CHRISTIANS WERE HAPPY BECAUSE THEY WOULD BE SUFFERING THE SAME WAY JESUS HAD.

First in the arena was Saturninus who said he wanted to face several types of wild animal.

AND SO AT THE OUTSET OF THE CONTEST HE AND REVOCATUS WERE MATCHED WITH A LEOPARD, AND THEN WHILE IN THE STOCKS THEY WERE ATTACKED BY A BEAR.
AS FOR SATURUS, HE WANTED TO BE KILLED BY ONE BITE OF A LEOPARD BUT HE WAS FACED WITH A

WILD BOAR. THE GLADIATOR WHO HAD TIED HIM TO
THE ANIMAL WAS GORED BY THE BOAR AND DIED
A FEW DAYS AFTER THE CONTEST, WHEREAS
SATURUS WAS ONLY DRAGGED ALONG. THEN WHEN HE
WAS BOUND IN THE STOCKS AWAITING THE BEAR,
THE ANIMAL REFUSED TO COME OUT OF THE CAGES,
SO THAT SATURUS WAS CALLED BACK ONCE MORE
UNHURT.

None of the men were killed by the animals – the Romans
would have to try again later. Then it was the turn of the
women…

FOR THE YOUNG WOMEN, HILARIANUS HAD PREPARED
A MAD, HORNED COW. SO THEY WERE STRIPPED NAKED,
PLACED IN NETS AND THUS BROUGHT OUT INTO THE
ARENA. EVEN THE CROWD WAS HORRIFIED WHEN
THEY SAW THAT SO THEY WERE BROUGHT BACK
AGAIN AND DRESSED IN UNBELTED TUNICS.

FIRST THE COW TOSSED PERPETUA AND SHE FELL ON
HER BACK. THEN, SITTING UP, SHE PULLED DOWN THE
TUNIC THAT WAS RIPPED ALONG THE SIDE SO THAT IT
COVERED HER THIGHS. NEXT SHE ASKED FOR A PIN
TO FASTEN HER UNTIDY HAIR: FOR IT WAS NOT RIGHT
THAT A MARTYR SHOULD DIE WITH HER HAIR IN
DISORDER.

Imagine that! You are about to die and you are worried about
your hairstyle?!

> THEN SHE GOT UP. AND SEEING THAT FELICITAS HAD BEEN CRUSHED TO THE GROUND, SHE WENT OVER TO HER, GAVE HER HAND, AND LIFTED HER UP. THEN THE TWO STOOD SIDE BY SIDE.

Saturus was brought back and attacked by a leopard that tore at him and left him bleeding.

> SHORTLY AFTER HE WAS THROWN WITH THE REST IN THE USUAL SPOT TO HAVE HIS THROAT CUT. BUT THE CROWD ASKED THAT THEIR BODIES BE BROUGHT OUT INTO THE OPEN SO THEY COULD SEE THE THROATS BEING CUT. AND SO THE MARTYRS GOT UP AND WENT TO THE SPOT AND KISSED ONE ANOTHER. SATURUS, BEING THE FIRST CLIMB THE STAIRWAY, WAS THE FIRST TO DIE.

But Perpetua didn't die easily. The Roman soldier was so nervous he hacked at her neck but failed to kill her…

> SHE SCREAMED AS SHE WAS STRUCK ON THE BONE; THEN SHE TOOK THE TREMBLING HAND OF THE YOUNG GLADIATOR AND GUIDED IT TO HER THROAT.

The Christians became 'martyrs' – heroes and heroines who died so bravely they made thousands of others want to copy them. Killing Christians in the arena didn't kill off the Christian Church. It only made it stronger.

Beaten but never beaten

The Romans enjoyed watching criminals being executed in the arena. But they seemed to hate Christians even more than robbers and murderers. Many Romans believed the Christians were cannibals. Sometimes games were arranged especially for Christian executions, and they often thought up hideous new tortures for the Christians before they killed them…

1 A Roman citizen who became a Christian, and was caught, was given a 'kinder' punishment than a common person. They would be beheaded. The common Christians were strangled in jail or thrown to the wild animals in the arena.
2 Death in the arena could be very slow – sometimes the Christians survived for days. Here's how the Christian writer Eusebius described some executions in Lyon…

Maturus, Sanctus, Blandina and Attalus were led into the arena and whipped. To crown it all they were put in a hot iron seat, from which their roasting flesh filled the audience with its scent. They were sacrificed after a day of suffering. Blandina was hung from a post as bait for wild animals to tear. None of the animals would touch her.

On the last day of the games Blandina was brought back. After the whips, the animals and the burning seat she was thrown in a net and shown to a wild bull. It tossed her to death but still the show was not finished. The crowd wanted to see the bodies torn apart.

3 The Romans made the living Christians suffer still further. They would not let their friends be buried, which meant

279

that their souls wouldn't go to heaven. Eusebius wrote this ... but a few of the words seem to have been cut out of the script. That's the trouble with these old diaries. Can you put the words back in the right places to tell the terrible truth?

THE CHRISTIANS WHO HAD BEEN [ ] IN PRISON WERE [ ] TO THE DOGS. GUARDS [ ] THEM DAY AND NIGHT TO MAKE SURE WE DIDN'T HAVE THE BODIES [ ]. SOME ROMANS [ ] ANGRY CURSES AT THE BODIES. OTHERS [ ] AND MOCKED THEM. SO THE BODIES OF THE MARTYRS WERE LEFT [ ] FOR SIX DAYS AND THE REMAINS WERE [ ] TO ASHES.

The missing words, not in order, are: buried, laughed, unburied, thrown, screamed, strangled, burned, watched.

Answers: strangled, thrown, watched, buried, screamed, laughed, unburied, burned.

4 Christians were blamed for *any* disaster that happened to Rome. If there was a plague in the city then the Romans knew the answer...

CHRISTIANS TO THE LIONS!

5 Saint Lawrence was able to have a laugh about his execution. He was roasted on a grill over a fire. After a while he told his torturer…

I think I'm done now. Eat a slice of flesh and let me know if it tastes good.

6 The Christians drank wine and believed it was the blood of Christ. But they had other uses for wine too:
- In AD 265 the Romans burned Fructuosus and some priests in an arena. Their Christian friends took jars of wine to the arena that night and used the wine to put out the flames.
- At Ankara, in Turkey, Theodorus was executed. His body should have been burned to stop his friends burying it. But a priest took wine into the prison and gave it to the guards. When they were drunk the priest stole the body of Theodorus.

The more the Romans killed them, the stronger the Christians became. After all, the first Christian, Jesus Christ, had been horribly killed by the Romans on a cross. Many Christians followed him and died horribly – but that just made *more* and *more* people want to copy their bravery.

In the end the Christians won. There were so many of them they were able to take over and stop the horrors of the Roman way of life – and the Roman ways of death.

Epilogue

The Romans lived in savage times. They had better roads and laws and weapons and leaders than their enemies – the people they called the 'Barbarians'. And the ancient Romans are rightly remembered for their cleverness – so clever we can look back at their history and still be amazed. Look at their ruins and wonder how they built such great things as Hadrian's Wall or the Colosseum 2,000 years ago. Just don't be blinded by their cleverness. The real secret of their success was that they could be more savage than their cruellest enemies. Totally ruthless Romans.

The English poet Lord Byron (1788–1824) looked around the ruin of the Colosseum and wrote that in that place...

Murder breathed her bloody steam.

Spot on, Byron. Not 'games'. Not 'sport'. *Murder*.

Even today some of the best Roman ideas stay with us – but, sadly, so do some of the worst bits of ancient Rome. We'll never know exactly how many Christians were executed in ancient Rome – but it's certain that far *more* Christians lost their lives for their religion in the last half of the 20th century!

It's sad that some things never change. Humans can still be every bit as vicious as they were 2,000 years ago. Sometimes it's hard to spot the difference between the ruthless 1st century and the ruthless 21st century. Here's an example...

CASE 1

A cruel ruler allowed no one to oppose him. One man who did struggle against the ruler was executed. As his corpse was thrown aside, the man's faithful dog stayed beside it and guarded it, heartbroken.

The place: Ancient Rome
The cruel ruler: Emperor Tiberius
The victim: Sabinus
The dog: Unknown
The date: AD 35

CASE 2

A cruel ruler allowed no one to oppose him. One man who did struggle against the ruler was executed. As his corpse was thrown aside, the man's faithful dog stayed beside it and guarded it, heartbroken.

The place: Zimbabwe
The cruel ruler: President Mugabe
The victim: Terry Ford, a 53-year-old farmer
The dog: Squeak
The date: 17 March 2002

The world changes. When will ruthless humans change?

MURDER, DICTATORS, BRUTAL CRIME AND LIONS

BOOK ON ROME?

NOPE. IT'S THE GUIDE FOR TONIGHT'S TV

Evil emperors

It's really weird but true. Some of the battiest people in history have been leaders – kings and queens, emperors and empresses, presidents and princes. It's almost as if you *have to be* slightly potty to be a ruler!

Rome had their fair share of rotten rulers. Here are a few foul facts about them. Only the odd word has been left out for you to complete…

Missing words in the wrong order: mother, head, chicken, horse, corpse, cobweb, cheese, wife, wrinkly, leg.

1 AUGUSTUS CAESAR (31 BC–AD 14) CAUGHT BRUTUS, THE MURDERER OF JULIUS CAESAR, AND HAD HIS _____ THROWN AT THE FEET OF CAESAR'S STATUE.

2 TIBERIUS (AD 14–37) SAID THAT HE WOULD SMASH THE _____ OF ANYONE WHO DISOBEYED HIM.

3 CALIGULA (AD 37–41) WANTED SOMEONE TO HELP HIM TO RULE SO HE GAVE THE JOB TO HIS _____.

4 CLAUDIUS (AD 41–54) HAD HIS _____ EXECUTED.

5 NERO (AD 54–68) TRIED TO DROWN HIS _____.

6 VITELLIUS (AD 69) HAD HIS _____ THROWN IN THE RIVER TIBER AT ROME.

7 HADRIAN (AD 117–138) FORCED A _____ TO COMMIT SUICIDE.

8 ANTONIUS (AD 138–161) DIED OF EATING TOO MUCH _____.

9 ELIOGABALUS (AD 218–222) HAD THE CURIOUS HOBBY OF COLLECTING EVERY _____ HE COULD FIND.

10 HONORIUS (AD 395–423) HAD A _____ CALLED 'ROME'.

Stabbing Jules

Julius Caesar was a brilliant Roman leader, but he became a bit too big for his boots – his red boots, in fact. The Romans were now used to having leaders who were 'elected'. They had hated their old kings … who had worn red boots instead of a crown, but when the booted-up kings were kicked out the Romans got on much better with their elected leaders.

But Julius got himself elected for life. Just like a king. When he started wearing red boots, his number was up. There was just one way to get rid of him then – assassination.

His friend Brutus led the murderers, who struck when Caesar was entering the Roman parliament (the senate). Roman writer Plutarch told the gory story. Can you sort out the scrambled words in this version?

Some of Brutus's gang slipped behind Caesar's chair while others came to meet him. Cimber grabbed Caesar's robe and pulled it from his neck. This was the **A SLING** for the attack.

Casca struck the first blow. His **IF KEN** made a wound in **ASS ACRE** neck but Caesar was able to turn round, grab the knife and hold on. The **HAT CREWS** were horrified but didn't dare move or make a sound.

Each **AS SINS AS** bared his dagger now. They pushed Caesar this way and that like a wild **BE SAT** surrounded by hunters.

Brutus stabbed Caesar in the groin. Above all Caesar had **RED TUTS** Brutus. When he saw Brutus coming towards him he pulled his robe over his head and sank down.

The attackers pushed Caesar against the **ASTUTE** of his old enemy Pompey. The statue became drenched with **DO LOB**.

Caesar received 23 wounds. Many of the assassins **WON DUDE** each other as they fought to stick so many knives into one body.

Many of the assassins wounded each other as they fought to stick so many knives into one body! Julius Caesar received a total of twenty-three wounds. Spot nine bloody differences between the two pictures and circle them with a pencil.

288

Funny 'n' foul emperor facts

Can you work out which of these weird emperor facts are true and which are false?

1 You could be executed for saying the word 'goat' near Caligula.

2 Claudius usually had a runny nose.

3 A doctor saved Claudius from poisoning by making him vomit with a feather.

4 Nero played the fiddle and watched while Rome burned.

5 Otho (AD 69) used wet bread as after-shave.

6 Commodus (AD 180–192) enjoyed shooting the heads off ostriches with his bow and arrow.

7 In AD 217 Empress Julia Domna stuffed herself with so much food that she burst.

8 Eliogabalus made his ministers carry sheep guts to the temple as a gift for the gods.

9 Gordian (AD 238) hanged himself with his shoelaces.

10 Victorinus (AD 269–271) was killed for chatting up a soldier's wife.

Awful army

The Romans were famous for their army. They were well organized and well armed. They were also mainly foreigners. The conquered peoples around the empire joined the Roman army and conquered other peoples who joined the Roman army and conquered ... and so on until they ran out of conkers.

But how much of the terrible truth do you know about these super soldiers?

1 If you were a beaten tribesman but refused to fight in the Roman army what could happen to you?
a) You would be forced to do all the washing up for the Roman army.
b) You would have your hair cut off so everyone could see you were a coward.
c) You would have your head cut off so everyone could see what happened to trouble-makers.

2 What did the Roman soldier wear under his leather kilt?
a) nothing
b) a fig leaf
c) underpants

  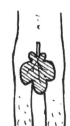

3 Who paid for a soldier's food, uniform, weapons ... and burial?
a) The emperor paid for everything.
b) The general paid for his soldiers out of his wages.
c) The soldier paid for himself out of his wages.

4 If you joined the Roman army how long did you have to stay in it?
a) 3 years
b) 25 years
c) 40 years

5 What would you use instead of toilet paper in the army toilets?
a) your underpants
b) a sponge on a stick
c) your sword

290

6 Who could a Roman soldier marry?
a) no one
b) a slave
c) a Roman

7 How tall did you have to be to be a Roman soldier?
a) under 1.6 metres
b) between 1.6 and 1.8 metres
c) over 1.8 metres

8 One Roman centurion was known as 'Give me another'. Why?
a) He was a greedy turnip and ate one chicken after another, always crying, 'Give me another!'
b) He was a sad bloke crying 'Give me my mother!' but his deaf soldiers heard him wrongly.
c) He was a bully who cried, 'Give me another!' every time he smashed a stick over a soldier as he beat him.

9 Roman spear-heads snapped off when they hit something. Why?
a) They were made of rubbish British iron.
b) The Romans made them to break off.
c) They weren't real spears, they were just for show.

10 An army doctor would treat you and not hear your screams. Why not?
a) He was trained not to listen.
b) His eardrums were burst as part of his doctor training.
c) Doctors were forbidden to wash ear wax out of their ears.

JUST ROMAN AROUND

Grotty graffiti

Graffiti looks pretty messy but it isn't a modern problem. There has been graffiti ever since humans could write … sort of 'Ug was here, one million years BC.'

The Romans had graffiti. How do we know? Because in AD 79 the Roman town of Pompeii was smothered in ash when the volcano Vesuvius erupted. Hundreds of years later the ruins were dug up and the graffiti was uncovered. Here are the sort of things those Romans wanted you to know…

CHIE OPTO TIBI UT REFRIGENT SE FICUS TUAE
Chie, I hope your piles rub themselves raw.

C PUMIDUS DIPILUS HEIC FUIT A D V NONAS OCTOBREIS M LEPID Q CATUL COS
Gaius Pumidius Dipilus was here, 3 December 78 BC.

MIXIMUS IN LECTO. SI DICES: QUARE? NULLA FUIT MATELLA
We have peed in our beds… If you ask: why? There was no potty.

EPAPHRODITUS CUM THALIA HAC
Epaphroditus was here with Thalia.

SAMIUS CORNELIOS SUSPENDRE
Samius to Cornelius: Go hang yourself!

CACATOR CAVE MALUM, AUT SI CONTEMPSERIS, HABEAS IOVEM IRATUM
Watch it, you that dumps in this place! May you have Jove's anger if you ignore this.

SUSPIRIUM PUELLARUM CELADUS THRAEX
Celadus the Thracian gladiator makes the girls sigh!

AUGII AMAT ALLOTENUM
Auge loves Allotenus.

PITUITA ME TENET
I've caught a cold.

VIRGULA TERTIO SUO INDECENS ES
Virgula to her boyfriend Tertius: You're disgusting!

ADMIROR PARIES TE NON CECIDISSE RUINIS QUI TOT SCRIPTORUM TAEDIAE SUSTINEAS
I am amazed, wall, that you have not fallen in ruins.

Gruesome games

It wasn't just the Roman emperors who were rotten. The people were pretty nasty, too! Murder was made into a 'sport'. Men and women were killed for fun. The idea of fighting and killing as a game probably began at funerals…

People believed that the souls of the dead were kept happy with human blood, so they sacrificed prisoners of war or slaves at funerals. But it was more fun to watch those victims fight for their lives. The funeral fights became so popular that they were moved out of graveyards and into huge arenas. The greatest arena was the Colosseum in Rome. This arena held 50,000 bloodthirsty Romans. Look carefully and work out which of the numbered pictures below are part of the Colosseum.

Choose your gladiator

Gladiators weren't all exactly the same. There were all sorts of different types. Here are a few you might like to try copying… using a rolled-up newspaper as a weapon, of course.

But first, can you match the gladiator to his title? But beware! To make it extra tricky there are *two* fake names in there!

1 ANDABATAE - CLUE: NEED A GUIDE DOG
2 DIMACHERI - CLUE: AMBIDEXTROUS ?
3 ORDINARII - CLUE: PLAIN AND SIMPLE
4 SPINACHERI - CLUE: TRAINED, LIKE POPEYE ON SPINACH
5 HOPLOMACHI - CLUE: GOOD KNIGHT ?
6 LAQUEATORES - CLUE: NO NOOSE IS BAD NOOSE
7 RETIARII - CLUE: THEY HAD A POINT — OR MORE
8 BEEFABURGI - CLUE: KILLS BULLS FOR THE EMPERORS BURGERS
9 SECUTORES - CLUE: SHIELDED
10 BESTIARII - CLUE: BEASTLY

MOO!

BING
BING

295

Gory gladiators

A Roman writer said…

> *Gladiators were men who fought with swords in the amphitheatre and other places for the amusement of the Roman people.*

Another Roman writer, Seneca, went to see the Roman 'games'. Fill in the gaps to find out what he wrote.

Missing words, not in the correct order: butchery, lions, death, robbers, sport, entertainment, murderers, spectators, winners, swords.

I HAPPENED TO DROP IN ON THE MIDDAY SPORT IN THE ARENA. I WAS LOOKING FOR A LITTLE (1) _____ BUT SAW ONLY (2) _____, PURE AND SIMPLE. THE FIGHTERS HAVE NOTHING TO PROTECT THEM. THEIR BODIES ARE OPEN TO EVERY BLOW, AND EVERY BLOW FINDS ITS MARK. THEY ARE LASHED FORWARD SO THEY CAN'T ESCAPE THE (3) _____.

IN THE MORNING MEN FIGHT (4) _____ AND BEARS, AT NOON THEY FIGHT EACH OTHER. THE (5) _____ FIGHT AGAIN AND AGAIN UNTIL THEY ARE DEFEATED. (6) _____ IS THE FIGHTER'S ONLY WAY OUT. THE (7) _____ SAY, 'BUT THESE MEN ARE HIGHWAY (8) _____ AND (9) _____. THEY DESERVE ALL THEY ARE GETTING!' CAN'T YOU SEE HOW WRONG THIS (10) _____ IS?

Seneca was banned from Rome for eight years for daring to say that about Emperor Caligula's sport! (Don't feel too sorry for Seneca – he was not a nice man!)

Gladiators wore armour to protect themselves when fighting – a GALEA (helmet with a visor), a GALERUS (metal shoulder piece), a MANICAE (leather bands on elbow or wrist) and an OCREA (shin guard of metal or boiled leather). They also used different weapons – a FASCINA (harpoon), a GLADIUS (sword), a HASTA (lance), an IACULUM (net), a PARMA (round shield), a SCUTUM (large oblong shield) and a SICA (curved sword). Find the words in CAPITALS above in the wordsearch. The words are written across, up, down, diagonally, forwards or backwards.

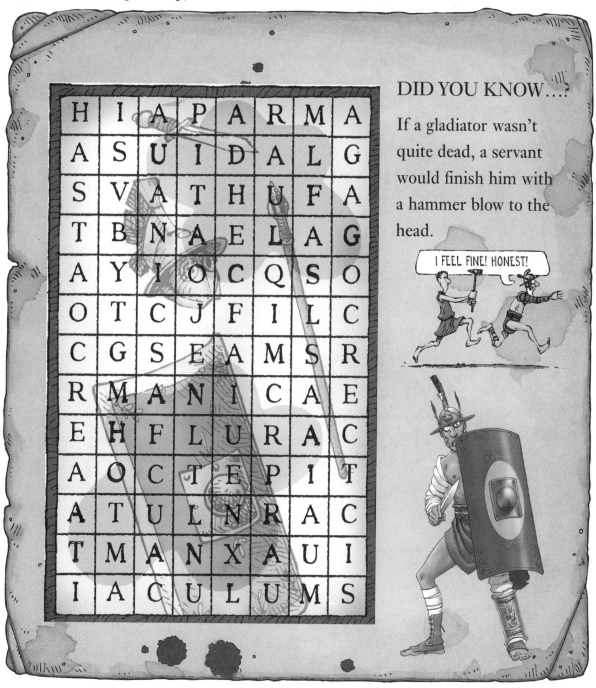

H	I	A	P	A	R	M	A
A	S	U	I	D	A	L	G
S	V	A	T	H	U	F	A
T	B	N	A	E	L	A	G
A	Y	I	O	C	Q	S	O
O	T	C	J	F	I	L	C
C	G	S	E	A	M	S	R
R	M	A	N	I	C	A	E
E	H	F	L	U	R	A	C
A	O	C	T	E	P	I	T
A	T	U	L	N	R	A	C
T	M	A	N	X	A	U	I
I	A	C	U	L	U	M	S

DID YOU KNOW…?

If a gladiator wasn't quite dead, a servant would finish him with a hammer blow to the head.

I FEEL FINE! HONEST!

Fearsome fighters

Gladiators were supposed to fight hard and put on a good show for the audience. But one group shocked Emperor Caligula when they refused to fight. Put the pictures in the right order to find out what happened…

Fill in the grid with the correct order.

F							

Caligula called it 'murder' and he probably had the Retiarii executed anyway. But at least they must have had a bit of a chuckle before they died!

298

Gladiators were not the only ones to fight in the arenas. Criminals did as well. They dressed like gladiators but the Romans knew they were not the real things. Those criminals (called 'noxii') gave the Romans all the blood and death they wanted to see and they were cheap. The real gladiators cost a lot of money to feed and train. Gladiators were not cheap slaves to be wasted.

> *Not everyone thought that killing people for fun was a great day out. The Roman writer, Seneca, went to see the Roman games and saw the 'noxii', doomed to die. Fill in the gaps to find out what he wrote…*

Missing words not in the correct order: fighters, defeated, murderers, sport, wrong, escape, bodies

I HAPPENED TO DROP IN ON THE MIDDAY ☐ IN THE ARENA. I WAS LOOKING FOR A LITTLE ENTERTAINMENT BUT SAW ONLY BUTCHERY, PURE AND SIMPLE. THE ☐ HAVE NOTHING TO PROTECT THEM. THEIR ☐ ARE OPEN TO EVERY BLOW, AND EVERY BLOW FINDS ITS MARK. THEY ARE LASHED FORWARD SO THEY CAN'T ☐ THE SWORD. IN THE MORNING MEN FIGHT LIONS AND BEARS, AT NOON THEY FIGHT EACH OTHER. THE WINNERS FIGHT AGAIN AND AGAIN UNTIL THEY ARE ☐ DEATH IS THE FIGHTER'S ONLY WAY OUT. THE SPECTATORS SAY, 'BUT THESE MEN ARE HIGHWAY ROBBERS AND ☐ . THEY DESERVE ALL THAT THEY ARE GETTING!' CAN'T YOU SEE HOW ☐ THIS SPORT IS?

Awful for animals

Want some fun in ancient Rome? Then get an animal to fight against a gladiator or against another animal. Even if the animal won, hunters or dogs then killed them. But some animals became favourites of the crowd. They fought bravely and the crowd decided they should live. One rhinoceros fought so well the crowd loved it. The rhino fought time and again in the arena for emperors Titus and Domitian. Work out which small picture matches the big one in the middle.

Rotten Roman punishment

The Romans were famous for making laws. It is said that Roman law was the start of most laws we still have today. But that doesn't mean the Roman laws were fair or free of cruelty. They weren't! If anyone tries to tell you the Romans had 'modern' laws, just remind them it was the Romans who liked to nail criminals to crosses.

In AD 64 there was a huge fire that destroyed a large area of Rome. The Romans were angry and looking for someone to blame. Emperor Nero accused a group of Jews who followed the teachings of Jesus: the Christians. He started executing them and the Romans enjoyed the idea.

History of Rome by Tacitus
Book 15, AD 62–65

Mockery of every sort was added to their deaths. They were covered with the skins of wild beasts, and then they were torn to death by **a) vultures/dogs/crocodiles** or were nailed to **b) crosses/wheels/trees** or were thrown to the **c) bottom of the sea/flames/pigs** and burnt, to serve as flaming **d) torches/fairy lights/candles** when darkness fell. Nero offered his gardens for the executions, and was putting on a show in the **e) bath/circus/vomitorium** while he mixed with the people in the dress of a **f) taxi/white van/chariot** driver.

Choose the correct word from the options labelled a) to f) above to read what the Roman historian, Tacitus wrote.

KILL YOURSELF, BEFORE I HAVE YOU EXECUTED

Painful punishment

Romans often tried to make a punishment fit a crime. If you were a poacher who stole someone else's deer, you may be sewn into the skin of the deer then set free. After a while hunting dogs would be sent after you. They would think you were a deer (because dogs are a bit stupid like that) and they would tear you to pieces. Lead this hungry dog through the Roman maze to the criminal hiding in the centre.

DID YOU KNOW…?

The Romans used hooks on hated criminals because they believed they were 'unclean' – no one wanted to touch their dead bodies.

Can you match the crime to the punishment? It would be criminal if you got too many wrong. So, anyone who gets less than four out of six can punish themselves by writing 100 times: 'I am not verrey brite.'

CRIME

PUNISHMENT

1) STEALING CROPS

A) NO PUNISHMENT

2) TELLING LIES ABOUT SOMEONE IN COURT

D) THROWN OFF THE TARPEIAN

3) MURDERING YOUR WIFE BECAUSE SHE DRINKS WINE

E) BURNED ALIVE

4) SETTING FIRE TO YOUR NEIGHBOUR'S HOUSE (ARSON)

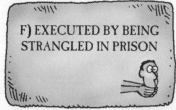
F) EXECUTED BY BEING STRANGLED IN PRISON

5) CALLING SOMEONE A NASTY NAME (SLANDER)

B) WALLED UP ALIVE

6) HAVING A BABY- IF YOU ARE A PRIESTESS

C) CLUBBED TO DEATH

Foul Roman food

Romans loved food. The rich could afford all sorts – the poor, as usual in history, ate whatever they could get their choppers round.

Do you know what the rotten Romans ate? Have a go at this quirky quiz on cuisine (that's a posh word for 'cooking') and find out…

1 The Romans didn't have tomato ketchup but they did have sauce made from what?
a) sheep eyeballs
b) fish guts
c) elephant's tail

2 At posh Roman feasts guests ate more than their stomachs could hold. How?
a) They emptied their stomachs by vomiting every now and then.
b) They stretched their stomachs with special exercises.
c) They stuck a pin in their stomach to let out trapped air and let in more food.

3 Snails were fattened up before they were killed. They were kept in a bowl of what?
a) chopped cabbage
b) brains
c) blood

4 Emperor Eliogabalus served 600 of them at one feast. What?
a) ostrich brains
b) ducks' feet
c) camel-burgers

5 Emperor Eliogabalus also served a meal where the peas were mixed with what?
a) queues
b) poison
c) gold nuggets

6 A Roman called Trimalchio had a feast with a roasted boar. When it was sliced down the belly, what came out?

a) maggots

b) songbirds

c) a dancing girl

7 What could you watch as you ate at some Roman feasts?

a) television

b) two gladiators trying to murder one another

c) tap-dancing bears

8 The Romans ate cute little pets that you probably wouldn't eat. What?

a) cats

b) budgies

c) dormice

9 The Romans did *not* eat animals' what?

a) teeth

b) brains

c) lungs

10 Emperor Maximian was a strange eater. Why?

a) He was the only vegetarian emperor.

b) He ate only eggs and drank only water.

c) He ate 20 kilos of meat a day.

Funny funerals

Here are ten questions about rotten Roman funerals. Can you guess which of the answers is correct?

1 A Roman law said women at funerals must not…
a) eat sweets as they walked down the street behind the coffin
b) tear at their cheeks with their fingernails to show how unhappy they were

2 To save themselves suffering the awful smell of a dead body the mourners…
a) wore clothes pegs on their noses
b) covered the corpse in sweet spices and perfumes

3 The writer Ovid said funerals were…
a) good places to chat up girls
b) bad places for catching colds

4 At the funeral of Julius Caesar the people watched…
a) a mechanical dummy revolving to show the 23 stab wounds
b) a fly-past of 23 trained pigeons

5 Caesar's funeral was unusual because it was…
a) held twice when a rainstorm put out the funeral fire at the first try
b) held in the city and not in the countryside even though that was against the law

6 Bodies were carried to funerals…
a) standing up
b) lying down

7 A Roman boy died and was cremated, and then his mother had a funeral because…
a) she heard about the death too late and missed the cremation
b) she enjoyed the first one so much she wanted to do it all over again

8 Not all Romans were cremated or buried, some were turned into mummies by…
a) soaking the body in honey
b) stuffing the body with cotton-wool

9 When the son of Roman Regulus died his father threw…
a) all of the boy's ponies, dogs and birds on to the funeral fire
b) himself on to the funeral fire

10 After a funeral the guests would sit by the graveside and…
a) have a laugh
b) have a meal

DID YOU KNOW…?
Roman army doctors didn't know about anaesthetics (to put you to sleep while they hacked you about!). They were trained not to hear your screams when they treated you.

NEXT!

Grisly quiz

Why not pester your parents and find out how much they know about the rotten Romans with this quick quiz?

1 In AD 64 Rome had a great fire. Emperor Nero blamed the Christians. How did he punish them? (Clue: let the punishment fit the crime!)

2 Why were there no dead bodies in Rome? Well, not for more than a couple of days. (Clue: they weren't buried in the dead centre of Rome)

3 Roman kids used a bit of a pig for a ball. What bit did they use? (Clue: a load of tripe)

4 If a gladiator fell but wasn't quite dead then a servant finished him off. How? (Clue: that's hitting the nail on the head)

5 A poisonous Roman spider bites you. You crush its body into the wound to cure it. But what do you use if you can't catch the spider? (Clue: search the internet)

6 The Romans cut off Saint Alban's head for being a Christian. As Alban's head hit the ground the executioner clutched at his own eyes. Why? (Clue: that's what you do when pupils fall out)

7 What did rich Romans do if a tooth fell out? (Clue: not true)

8 A father was the ruler of the family. What was the harshest punishment he could give a wicked son? (Clue: the son would never be wicked again!)

9 In AD 71 Spartacus led a slave rebellion. It ended when 6,000 slaves were executed along the side of a road. How did they die? (Clue: they were very cross.)

10 Chariot races were between four teams – reds, greens, blues and whites. They often caused fights to break out. Who fought? (Clue: too easy to need a clue!)

Answers

Evil Emperors

1 Head. Nice present for Jules!

2 Leg. Tiberius died at the age of 78, probably suffocated by his chief helper.

3 Horse. Cruel Caligula liked to feed criminals to wild animals. He was stabbed to death by one of his guards.

4 Wife. She was a bit of a flirt. But he also had 300 of her party friends chopped too! His third wife, and niece, had him poisoned with mushrooms.

5 Mother. When the plot failed he sent soldiers to give her the chop. Nero stabbed himself to death before his enemies got to him.

6 Corpse. He was murdered in the centre of Rome but not given a nice emperor's burial.

7 Wrinkly. Hadrian accused Servianus of treason and forced him to kill himself. But Servianus was 90 years old and hardly a big threat.

8 Cheese. At least that's what a Roman historian blamed his death on. Guess it was just hard cheese.

9 Cobweb. Maybe he was planning to build the world's first web-site?

10 Chicken. Trouble is he loved the chicken Rome more than he loved the city Rome, and the city was neglected.

Stabbing Jules

These are the unscrabbled words in the correct order: signal; knife; Caesar's; watchers; assassin; beast; trusted; statue; blood; wounded.

Funny 'n' foul emperor facts

1 True. He was very hairy all over his body – like a goat. So he was very touchy and anyone saying the 'g' word would be executed.

2 True. He was a bit of a mess all round. His head shook, his knees wobbled, his mouth foamed and his voice stammered.

3 False. The doctor was part of the plot to poison him. When the first lot of poison failed to kill Claudius the doctor offered to make him vomit by tickling his throat with a feather. But the feather was soaked in even *more* poison and finished Claudius off!

4 False. This is a popular story but it just isn't true. Nero wasn't in Rome when the fire started. When he heard about it he hurried back and organized the fire-fighting. Of course fiddles hadn't been invented, but Nero *did* play the lyre (probably very badly).

5 True. Don't ask me why, though. Emperors always seem to have had too much dough! His hair was so thin he wore a wig and had every hair of his body plucked out. Ouch!

6 True. He used wide-headed arrows. As the ostriches ran round in circles he sliced off their heads. The birds kept running round … like headless chickens!

7 False. She starved herself to death because she was afraid Emperor Macrinus would torture her.

8 True. He made important people, not the servants, carry the sheep and cattle guts as part of the daily sacrifices.

9 False. He hanged himself with his belt when he heard his son had been killed fighting for him. Gordian ruled for just 22 days.

10 True. He made a habit of it. The husbands got jealous. One got very jealous indeed and had a victorious fight with Victorinus.

Awful army

1c) You have to fight for Rome, which is a real pain in the neck. If you don't it's a *real* pain in the neck.

2c) Can you blame them? Go to Hadrian's Wall in winter and see how cold it gets. You'd want to wear five pairs of knickers!

3c) Paying for your own burial is a bit tough. If I were a dead Roman soldier I'd refuse to pay!

4b) Unless you were killed, of course, in which case you were in it for life!

5b) The sponge was dipped in water (cold), used, then rinsed and left for the next person. Hmmm! Try it next time you run out of a roll.

6a) At least, they weren't supposed to marry. But many soldiers had wives outside the camp.

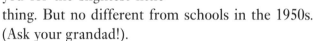
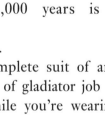

7b) But this rule was often broken if the army was desperate for men.

8c) It was a hard life when your centurion could beat you for the slightest little thing. But no different from schools in the 1950s. (Ask your grandad!).

9b) The idea was that they hit their enemy. But if they missed and the head snapped off, then the enemy couldn't throw them back.

10a) You may well have a school dentist a bit like that.

Gruesome games

3, 5 and 6 are not part of the Colosseum.
Fighters became known as gladiators.

Choose your gladiator

1j) These gladiators wore helmets with no eye slits – so they were fighting blindfold!

2c) These clever gladiators fought with two swords. So they couldn't have held a shield, of course. Once they'd cut through their enemy's defences, they must have been a bit like a food processor and made them into mincemeat.

3d) Now this may surprise you but they were ordinary gladiators. That is, they fought one-to-one with other ordinary ordinarii. You still have that sort of fighting in school playgrounds. To think it's been going on for 2,000 years is quite extraordinarii.

4g) Sorry, they didn't exist.

5i) They fought in a complete suit of armour. Sounds like the right sort of gladiator job to get. Imagine facing a lion while you're wearing the armour. Once he'd snapped his teeth and claws on your metal skin you could kill it. Cheating a bit, is that.

6f) These cowboy gladiators used a noose to capture their opponents. This sounds quite loopy.

7b) These gladiators fought with just a three-pointed lance (or trident) and a net. This is very useful if you're going fishing but a bit dangerous if you are up against a man with a sword.

8a) Sorry, no such thing.

9e) Gladiators armed with sword and shield, usually up against the retiarius with his net. If he missed with the net you chased him and tried to kill him.

10h) These were people who fought against wild animals. If you were lucky you went to a beast-fighting school and learned how to kill them. You were given weapons and were expected to win and live.

Of course, not many of the gladiators wanted to go in to the arena and fight to the death ... and who can blame them? So they were forced in by attendants carrying whips and red-hot irons.

If you were a criminal you were really unlucky – you'd be sent in unarmed. The beasts were expected to kill you, tear you apart and eat you. Don't try this at home with your pet poodle as you will make a terrible mess on the carpet and your parents will have to pay a fortune to have it cleaned.

Gory gladiators

1 entertainment; **2** butchery; **3** swords; **4** lions; **5** winners; **6** death; **7** spectators; **8** robbers; **9** murderers; **10** sport.

Gladiators wore armour

H	I	A	P	A	R	M	A
A	S	U	I	D	A	L	G
S	V	A	T	H	U	F	A
T	B	N	A	E	L	A	G
A	Y	I	O	C	Q	S	O
O	T	C	J	F	I	L	C
C	G	S	E	A	M	S	R
R	M	A	N	I	C	A	E
E	H	P	I	U	R	A	C
A	O	C	T	E	P	I	T
A	T	U	L	N	R	A	C
T	M	A	N	X	A	U	I
I	A	C	U	L	U	M	S

Fearsome Fighters
Correcet order: F E A D C G H B

Gladiators were not
Missing words in the correct order: SPORT, FIGHTERS, BODIES, ESCAPE, DEFEATED, MURDERERS, WRONG

Awful for animals
A matches the picture in the middle.

Rotten Roman punishments
a) dogs b) crosses c) flames d) torches e) circus f) chariot

Painful punishment

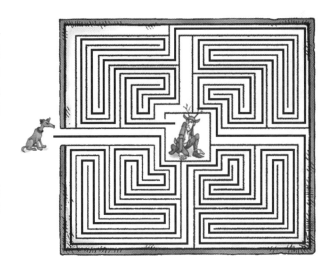

Can you match
1 = F   2 = D   3 = A   4 = E   5 = C
6 = B

Foul Roman food
1b) The guts were soaked in salt water and left to stew in the sun for a few days. Then the fish-gut sauce was poured over the food as a tasty treat. Oh my cod!

2a) They went to a special room called a vomitorium and threw up. They used a stick with a feather to tickle their tonsils and vomited into a bowl.

3c) The snails supped the blood till they were too fat to get in their shells. The blood diet made them taste nice. If they wanted creamy snails, the Romans fed them on milk before eating them.

4a) Ostrich brains are quite small so he'd need 600 to keep his guests fed. But where did he get all those ostriches? Zoo knows?

5c) Eliogabalus mixed gold and precious stones with the peas as a sort of treat.

6b) There were thrushes stuffed inside the roast boar. (Were they bored in there?)

7b) Of course, the trouble with gladiators fighting as you eat is that they could splash blood and guts all over your freshly cooked dinner.

8c) They fed the dormice really well on walnuts, acorns and chestnuts. They were served roasted and stuffed with pork sausage. Scrummy! Even tastier than hamster or gerbil!

9a) They ate all sorts of other things though. As well as sheep and goat lungs or brains, they ate gulls, peacocks, swans and jackdaws. They stuffed the birds just by pushing stuffing straight down their throats.

10c) That's about a small sheep every day.

Funny funerals

1b); 2b); 3a); 4a); 5b); 6a); 7a); 8a); 9a); 10b).
Caesar's wax dummy also had an actor speaking in Caesar's voice and naming the murderers. Creepy, eh? People reported seeing him going up to heaven. Hope they had plenty of mops in heaven to soak up all that blood!

Grisly Quiz

1 He burned them alive. Rome had seven fire brigades and they all failed to control the Great Fire.

2 They were all buried outside the city. Julius Caesar passed a law saying cremations and burials must take place outside the city. This was to keep diseases out of the city. Well, you wouldn't want a mouldy body in your back garden, would you?

3 The pig's stomach. They knotted it at each end, then blew it up. Would you fancy giving a kiss of life to a pig's belly? They played ball games like 'trigon' – rather like passing a balloon between three people.

4 With a hammer blow to the head. This was cleaner than a chop with a sword.

5 The spider's web. And crushed frogs drunk in wine are a good cure for toad-poison. It's no worse than some things you eat in burger bars.

6 His eyes fell out. At least that's what the legend says.

7 Got a false tooth. Romans made false teeth out of gold or ivory. And they kept their teeth clean using tooth powder. One tooth powder was made of mouse-brains – to keep their teeth squeaky clean?

8 Execution. Usually they made do with a good whipping or maybe sold the boy as a slave. But don't tell your parents this rotten Roman trick. It might give them ideas!

9 They were crucified. No one is quite sure if Spartacus was crucified or died in battle. But it's a great story that has been turned into books and films and computer games and even a ballet.

10 The fans. Just like modern soccer matches the fans had their favourites and the real boneheads wanted to give rival fans a kicking. Not a lot has changed in 2,000 years, has it?

313

TANKS A LOT!

HORRIBLE HISTORIES

WOEFUL SECOND WORLD WAR

TERRY DEARY ILLUSTRATED BY MARTIN BROWN

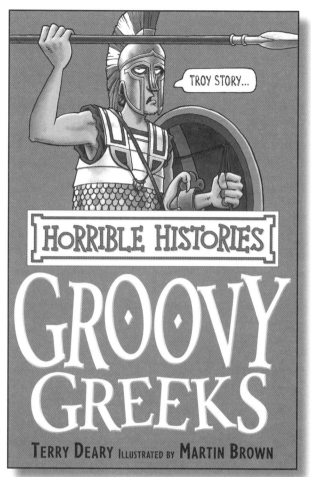

TROY STORY...

HORRIBLE HISTORIES

GROOVY GREEKS

TERRY DEARY ILLUSTRATED BY MARTIN BROWN

I'M GOING UP IN THE WORLD

HORRIBLE HISTORIES

VILE VICTORIANS

TERRY DEARY ILLUSTRATED BY MARTIN BROWN

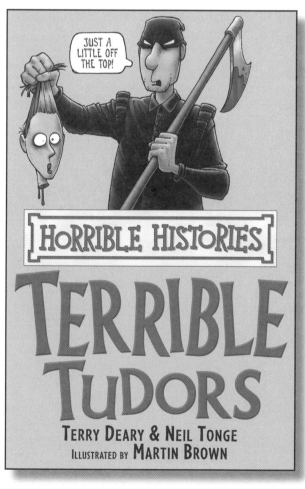

JUST A LITTLE OFF THE TOP!

HORRIBLE HISTORIES

TERRIBLE TUDORS

TERRY DEARY & NEIL TONGE ILLUSTRATED BY MARTIN BROWN

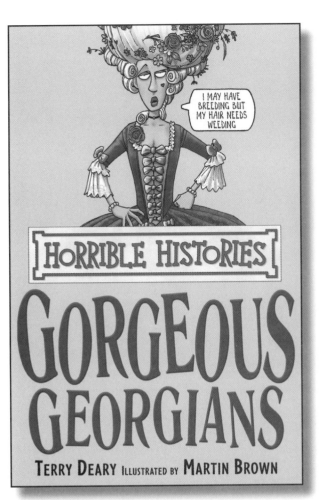

HORRIBLE HISTORIES

GORGEOUS GEORGIANS

TERRY DEARY ILLUSTRATED BY MARTIN BROWN

HORRIBLE HISTORIES

SMASHING SAXONS

TERRY DEARY ILLUSTRATED BY MARTIN BROWN

HORRIBLE HISTORIES

FRIGHTFUL FIRST WORLD WAR

TERRY DEARY ILLUSTRATED BY MARTIN BROWN

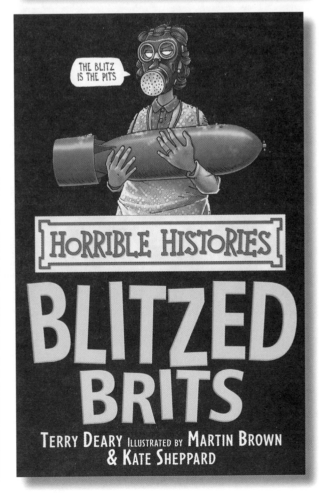

HORRIBLE HISTORIES

BLITZED BRITS

TERRY DEARY ILLUSTRATED BY MARTIN BROWN & KATE SHEPPARD

HORRIBLE HISTORIES
VICIOUS VIKINGS
TERRY DEARY ILLUSTRATED BY **MARTIN BROWN**

HORRIBLE HISTORIES
STORMIN' NORMANS
TERRY DEARY ILLUSTRATED BY **MARTIN BROWN**

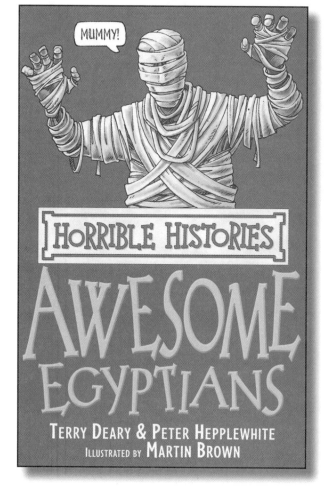

HORRIBLE HISTORIES
AWESOME EGYPTIANS
TERRY DEARY & PETER HEPPLEWHITE
ILLUSTRATED BY **MARTIN BROWN**

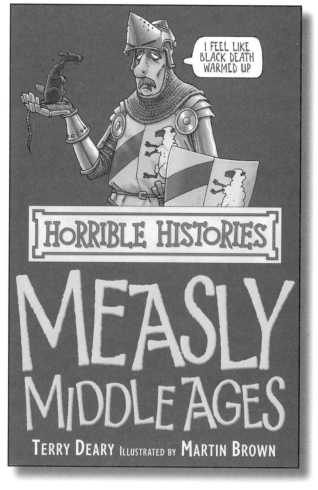

HORRIBLE HISTORIES
MEASLY MIDDLE AGES
TERRY DEARY ILLUSTRATED BY **MARTIN BROWN**

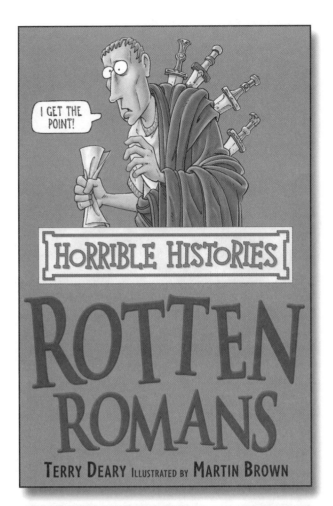

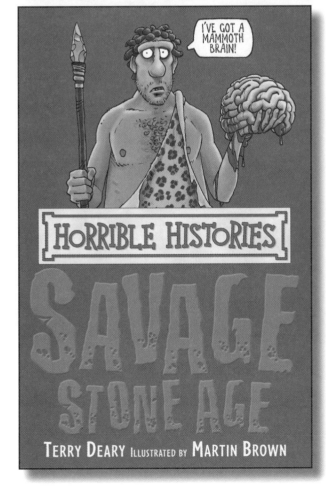

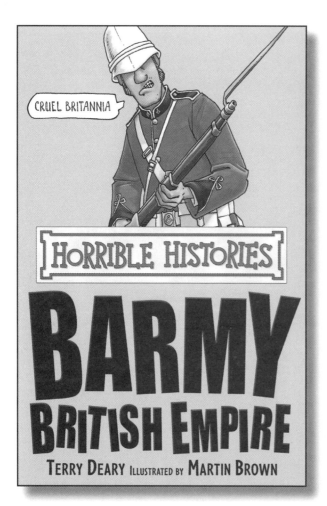

HORRIBLE HISTORIES

BARMY
BRITISH EMPIRE

TERRY DEARY ILLUSTRATED BY MARTIN BROWN

HORRIBLE HISTORIES

VILLAINOUS
VICTORIANS

TERRY DEARY ILLUSTRATED BY MARTIN BROWN

HORRIBLE HISTORIES

ANGRY
AZTECS

TERRY DEARY ILLUSTRATED BY MARTIN BROWN

HORRIBLE HISTORIES

INCREDIBLE
INCAS

TERRY DEARY ILLUSTRATED BY MARTIN BROWN
& PHILIP REEVE

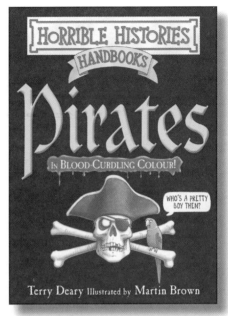

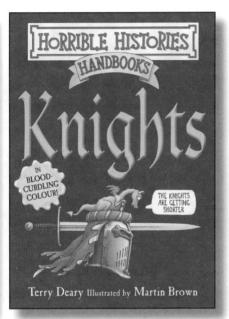

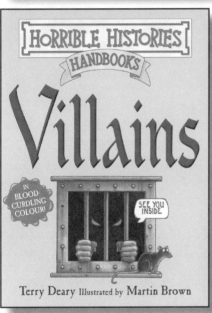

Don't miss these horribly handy handbooks for all the gore and more!